'There are books on church growth that are strong on principles and weak on application, others are full ... little theological rationale. Here Nick Cuthbert and ... balance with a book to stretch our ... and fire our hearts.'
Ian Coffey, Spring Harvest Leader, ... Crossroads Church Geneva

'I sometimes feel the Church is comatose, but the story in this book warmed my heart and give me hope that the Church is awakening. The principles in this book for a healthy church are wise and perceptive. I urge every church leader to read this book; it will inspire, encourage and motivate you. It certainly did that for me.'
J.John, Director The Philo Trust, author and evangelist

'An inspiration for mission possible. Here are new horizons for the imagination, thoughtful principles for the mind and compelling stories of God at work through people prepared to have a go, with him.'
Mark Greene, Executive Director London Institute for Contemporary Christianity

'The blend of sound principles and inspiring, real-life stories make *Church on the Edge* a compelling read and an invaluable resource for anyone with a heart for mission.'
Rob Parsons, Executive Director, Care for the Family

'Here is a kaleidoscope of ideas for people who mean business when it comes to opening up the Church for no-holds-barred mission. You don't have to agree with all of it and you certainly couldn't copy all the examples of how it has been done elsewhere. But please read it. My hope is that it will strip away any vestiges of religiosity and help you to be challenged by the Christ who is at the centre of mission. He called you to be his witness in the power of the Holy Spirit, as you offer yourself in worship. Pray for guidance and strength to do what is right where you are.'
The Most Revd and Rt. Hon. Dr John Sentamu, Archbishop of York

CHURCH ON THE EDGE
ENGAGING PRINCIPLES OF 21st CENTURY MISSION
Reaching the Unchurched Network

Chris Stoddard & Nick Cuthbert

Authentic

12 11 10 09 08 07 06   7 6 5 4 3 2 1

First published 2006 by Authentic Media
9 Holdom Avenue, Bletchley, Milton Keynes, Bucks, MK1 1QR, UK
and 129 Mobilization Drive, Waynesboro, GA 30830-4575, USA
www.authenticmedia.co.uk
Authentic Media is a division of Send the Light Ltd., a company limited by guarantee
(registered charity no. 270162)

British Library Cataloguing in Publication Data
A catalogue record for this book is available from theBritish Library

ISBN 1-86024-551-X

Cover design by Sam Redwood
Print Management by Adare Carwin
Printed in Great Britain by J.H. Haynes & Co., Sparkford

Contents

PART 2

ACKNOWLEDGEMENTS

We are grateful to the many people who have shared the journey with us as we have worked both individually and together on the content for this book. There are however some who we would like to thank specifically including Rick Miles, Chris Scupham, Helen Smith and John Butterworth for their proof reading, comments and suggestions. Also Lois Cuthbert and Liz Stoddard for their invaluable input, patience and support. We are of course indebted to all those who have been willing to contribute their stories, without which this book would not have been possible.

Chris Stoddard & Nick Cuthbert
February 2006

Introduction

This is a book of two halves; one a series of real life stories and the other containing some principles upon which they are based. The layout is designed for an easy read and gives the possibility of reading it in any order that is helpful to you.

To understand the philosophy behind it, let us share three metaphors.

1. SET THE SAIL . . . EXPECT THE WIND!

I have never been a great sailor but I have experienced the excitement of it. I do know three things:

- You will never go anywhere if you do not set the sails

- You will never go anywhere if there is no wind

- You cannot control the wind but you can hoist the sail

We all know that we shall achieve little without the power of the Holy Spirit bringing life to what we do. But the Bible is packed full of illustrations that show that when men did the possible, God did the impossible. Miracles always follow faith.

We cannot bring a spiritual turn-around in Europe, anymore than John Wesley on his horse could change England in the eighteenth century but we can be obedient to God and put some sails up. The sails depict a church that is setting itself to do what it was made to do. It was designed to continue the incarnation of Jesus. Its calling and its purpose is mission. The command of the great commission to make disciples is still the call on the church today. If God should bring an awakening, so much the better but we must do our part.

The question we must all ask today is whether we are safely in the harbour, tied to the jetty, sitting on the deck enjoying a cool drink and musing about how delightful the boating life is, or are we earnestly setting the sail ready to do things we were made to do?

This book is one attempt to give us some tools to set the sails and to move out of the comfort of the harbour into the adventure of the open sea.

2. CHANGE THE DNA

If DNA is the determining structure in the human body as to how we behave, then we will all inevitably respond physically to what is written down for us. If the DNA is 'faulty' it leads to disease. One of the great advances of modern science is the possibility to alter DNA so that the body grows differently. The church was built with certain DNA in its system but over time that seems to have been changed. In many places in the western world, it is now set to maintenance and survival. A superficial attempt to make changes on the surface will not do the job. What is required is a fundamental change of mindset at the most basic level; a change in the DNA.

3. RESET THE DEFAULT

In computer-speak, applications will always go back to the default setting even if they have been temporarily altered. For a permanent change in how the computer responds, you have to change the default settings. As with the DNA illustration, the present default of the church is set on pastoral care and maintaining what we have. Sudden flurries into mission will always default back. Individual Christians do not as a whole have 'mission' as default in their thinking. That is not a point of blame, it is the result of our history. But it is time to change the default of church life.

And so, this book is designed to help the process along the way. We recognise that there are no quick fix solutions and we are going to need to be in this for the long haul. The good news is that the process has in many cases well and truly begun and mission is back on the agenda.

This is designed to be an 'everyperson's' guide to mission church and is suitable for people at any level of church leadership or responsibility. It is not an 'arrival' book but for people on a journey written by fellow travellers.

It is deliberately designed to be closer to a manual than a book. We hope it is helpful.

PART 1

The times are changing

In the first part we will have a brief overview to look at some of the changes that are happening around us. It is essential we know something of the environment in which we are trying to be effective for the kingdom of God.

So we will look at . . .

- Christendom passing
- Modernity failing
- Secularisation growing
- Church attendance declining
- Spirituality thriving
- Society changing

危機

When written in Chinese, the word 'crisis' is composed of two characters. One represents danger and the other represents opportunity.

The times, they are a-changing!

These are confusing times to live in. If you like adventure you will find it exciting. If you prefer the settled life, this will be a very disturbing time as it is a period when something is finishing and the new has not yet appeared. When it does the old and the new will have to learn to live side by side in harmony.

Eddie Gibbs said to a group of leaders that we now have

> . . . a generation of leaders who do not know how to lead within a context of rapid and chaotic change. We were trained to map read on well-marked roads, not navigate on stormy seas. I believe the changes are significant and irreversible — while tomorrow continues to arrive ahead of schedule, yesterday can never be revisited.
> (*Quadrant* magazine, July 2001)

Brian McLaren in *The Church on the Other Side* (Zondervan, 2002), writes

> You and I happen to be born at an 'edge', at a time of high 'tectonic' activity in history — the end of one age and the beginning of another. It is a time of shaking. Yesterday's maps are outdated, and today's will soon be too.

This was tragically demonstrated by the devastating earthquake in Pakistan. Here was a whole community living on top of two shifting tectonic plates.

We need to note that movement in itself is not bad, in fact the physical world as we know it today has been shaped in this way over millions of years. Very few die from the actual earthquake, the problem is that people are living in structures that are inadequate and unprepared so that when foundations are shaken they collapse.

We are living in such a spiritual environment, change is all around and we are losing our reference points, the landscape is altering and we have no power over it. We can however change the way we live so that we can adapt to conditions around us. The church needs to take this very seriously if we are not to become completely irrelevant.

Times of transition

William Bridges, in his book *Managing Transitions* (Da Capo Press, 2003), uses the following helpful if a little dated illustrations of transition:

- It is like setting out by ship from one country to another. While the familiar shoreline disappears in the distance, the other may not yet have come into view. It is at that point you trust your compass is correct and your faith in the existence of the new land well founded.

- It is like the feeling that is experienced by Linus of *Peanuts* fame when his blanket is in the washing machine! Life can be difficult when your security blanket is taken away.

- It is the experience of the trapeze artist who lets go of his swing, trusting that his partner is coming at the right moment to catch him.

The generation who were born into the microchip revolution are used to the idea that 'constant change is here to stay'. But there are still a vast number of people who are reeling under the enormity and the speed at which so many changes are taking place. There is a tendency to believe that 'life will get back to normal' at some point. 'If we hold out long enough, they will bring back the typewriter, the dial telephone and letter post. It will all be back to how we knew it and could understand it!'

But there is no going back. There is no return.

We are in a time of huge flux not just in terms of technology but in our whole way of seeing and doing things. The word *culture* has been defined by some as *'how we do things around here'*! And 'how we do things' is changing and we would be wise to at least acknowledge that even if we do not know what to do about it.

The captain of a ship at sea who has lost sight of what is familiar relies on the security and sturdiness of his ship and the accuracy of his compass. Our safety is being 'in Christ' and our sure compass is God's word and our guide, the Holy Spirit. He is not fazed by the changes and we will find it an exciting adventure if we hold on tight to him.

SO WHAT ARE THESE CHANGES?

Most of the changes we are recounting are particular to the West and more especially to Western Europe. In most other parts of the globe the Christian church sails on at a pace. The purpose of mentioning these is not to give an in-depth analysis of our culture but to demonstrate that a lot of things are happening at once. The dominoes are falling one after the other.

Christendom passing

Christendom had its beginnings in the fourth century AD at the so-called conversion of the emperor, Constantine. It is a term that describes the intertwining of church and state. For centuries, this has affected the governmental, legal, institutional and artistic life of the nation and nations. Christianity became the overriding culture that influenced every part of national life. That is now passing in Western Europe. We are becoming 'post- Christendom'.

Post-Christendom, as defined by Stuart Murray in his book, *Post-Christendom* (Paternoster, 2004) is

> the culture that emerges as the Christian faith loses coherence within a society that has been definitively shaped by the Christian story and as the institutions that have been developed to express Christian convictions decline in influence.

Stuart puts forward a number of very helpful transitions that will take place during this period. For our purposes, they are well worth noting here:

- **From the centre to the margins**: in Christendom the Christian story and the churches were central, but in post-Christendom these are marginal.

- **From majority to minority**: in Christendom Christians were the (often overwhelming) majority, but in post-Christendom we are the minority.

- **From settlers to sojourners**: in Christendom Christians felt at home in a culture shaped by their story, but in post-Christendom we are aliens, exiles and pilgrims in a culture where we no longer feel at home.

- **From privilege to plurality**: in Christendom Christians enjoyed many privileges, but in post-Christendom we are one community among many in a plural society.

- **From control to witness**: in Christendom churches could exert control over society, but in post-Christendom we exercise influence only through witnessing to our story and its implications.

- **From maintenance to mission**: in Christendom the emphasis was on maintaining a supposedly Christian status quo, but in post-Christendom it is on mission within a contested environment.

- **From institution to movement**: in Christendom churches operated mainly in institutional mode, but in post-Christendom we must become again a Christian movement.

This may sound rather discouraging, but historically the Christian church has thrived in such an environment. Even though the process feels rapid and irreversible, it does not need to be a cause of despair. The kingdom of God remains unshakeable.

The main contrasts between Christendom and post-Christendom are worth pointing out here because they are directly related to what follows later.

PATTERNS OF CHURCH

IN CHRISTENDOM
- The church is structured pastorally and parochially
- The church expects people to come to it
- Mission predominantly happens on the margins
  (e.g. Anabaptists, John Wesley, Salvation Army, Pentecostals, Billy Graham, etc.)

IN POST-CHRISTENDOM
- The church comes from the margins as a mission group
- Parish boundaries break down
- The church expects to go out to where people are
- Mission comes out of the very heart of church life

PATTERNS OF LEADERSHIP

IN CHRISTENDOM

- Leadership is founded on a priestly model
- It is hierarchical
- It is clergy led and mostly controlling in nature

IN POST-CHRISTENDOM

- Leadership must be based on team ministries
- It must express body-life and ministry
- It must be releasing in nature
- It will express team rather than one person solo leadership

---

Note: Whilst we may be entering a whole new paradigm for church life, the old will be with us for some time yet, maybe always. Alongside, the new will emerge. New ideas and models must not be seen as superior to the old but without them we will lose touch with a large percentage of the population. We need whatever suits the situation best. Variety will be the key.

Modernity failing

No book on modern trends would be complete without a mention of that illusive thing called post-modernity. Again it describes something we are coming out of rather than what we will be in. Fundamentally, it reminds us that the way some (but by no means all) people see things today is not as they used to. The days when scientific rationalism dominated how we think is fast passing. Modernity has failed to answer all the questions. Some of the fundamental perceived changes in thinking are as follows:

- **Truth is relative**: 'What is true for you is fine but it isn't necessarily true for me.' This means that evangelism cannot be boiled down to purely a discussion of what is and what is not true.

- **No big story:** The Christian view that there is one overarching story is for some no longer acceptable. Rather it is that I have my story and you have yours. It means that the value of personal testimony is both easily accepted and an effective means of communicating.

- **Avoidance of belonging to institutions:** It is not just commitment to the church that is declining. It is true of most major political and social institutions as well.

- **No final authority:** People are less inclined to take anyone else's opinion as final – which includes the authority of the Bible.

- **Pick 'n' mix belief:** It is becoming acceptable to believe in a series of apparently inconsistent things at the same time. This might include having a belief in more than one religious system.

 Note: Whilst we may be entering a period where modernity is being challenged in people's thinking, this in no way describes all people. Therefore methods and approaches in evangelism must take into account that society is in flux and that just because a person is twenty-five years of age, does not mean they think and behave as a post-modern person or just because a person is over fifty they have not embraced post-modernity. It isn't that straightforward.

One of the positive sides of post-modernity is that people who in the past have been shy and reticent to talk about spiritual things find it a little more acceptable to do so. To believe in the 'spiritual' has become more socially acceptable.

Secularisation growing

Europe is experiencing a relentless process of 'creeping secularisation'. As Christendom fades, so secularism seeks to take its place.

In simple terms, secularisation describes what happens when reference to God and the spiritual side of humanity is elbowed out of public life. It is a belief that we can run the central tenets of society without the need for a belief in or a dependence on the divine. It is both the cause and the effect of the demise of Christendom.

In Grace Davie's must-read book, *Europe, the Exceptional Case* (Darton, Longman & Todd Ltd., 2002) she compares and contrasts what is happening in Europe with each of the other continents of the world. Her conclusion is that what makes Europe unique is that it has embraced secularism along with the processes of modernisation. She particularly points out the contrasts with the USA where the influence of the evangelical church is obvious. The contrast between Europe and the USA is an important one as many tend to look to the USA for patterns of church growth, often forgetting the huge difference in this regard. When Americans talk about reaching the 'unchurched', they predominantly mean those who once related to church who are coming back. In Europe the 'unchurched' means never having had any contact with church.

This contrast is becoming more and more apparent. The effects of secularisation are increasingly seen in Europe in government, media and education and in medical ethics.

 Note: If secularisation is a particularly European issue, we need to be very careful before we take models of church life or methods of evangelism from other continents. The attitudes, experience and beliefs of people in a secularised culture will be very different from those in another environment. What works for one place does not necessarily work for another place. The culture in which we are operating may require a very different approach.

> But human beings are made in the image of God and therefore cannot be secularised. Institutions can be secularised and people can think in a secular way but they will always be spiritual in their make-up. You can never take that away from them. Therein lies hope.

Church attendance declining

If the most commonly quoted statistics are even remotely correct, the church in Western Europe is in a serious crisis. There has been a steady and quite steep decline for over four decades. There are some mainstream denominations that, if present trends continue, will cease to exist in Britain in twenty-five years time. The majority (but by no means all) of churches are not growing and where they are it is extremely slow (unless you are part of a specific ethnic or national group, or people are joining you from other churches). Black and ethnic churches in Britain are the ones experiencing growth. The recent census may also reveal that in a number of areas, the Church of England is experiencing growth, particularly London, but in many places the situation has been serious for some time. The statistics are well documented in Peter Brierley's book, *The Tide is Running Out* (Christian Research, 2000).

Note: The statistics are based on church attendance. The huge change in patterns of church attendance i.e. regular attenders coming once a week but now many only going once a month with no less sense of commitment may mean that the statistics do not accurately reflect all that is going on. Also it should be noted that most major non-religious institutions are recording a decline in membership.

Callum Brown, in his book, *The Death of Christian Britain* (Routledge, 2001), paints a particularly gloomy picture of the future of Britain (and by association most of Europe). He cites the massive and seemingly unremitting church decline since the 1960s.

Although many would seriously debate the reasons he gives for this decline, some might agree with his concluding remarks

> This is not the death of churches, for despite their dramatic decline, they will continue to exist in some skeletal form with increasing commitment from decreasing numbers of adherents. Nor is it the death of belief in God, for though that too has declined, it may well remain as a root belief of people. But the culture of Christianity has gone in the Britain of the new millennium. Britain is showing the world how religion as we have known it can die.

It is Grace Davie who, as a subtitle to another book, *Religion in Britain Since 1945* (Blackwell Publishers 1994), coined the phrase 'believing without belonging'. She points out that the decline in church attendance across Europe does not indicate a loss of belief, even if the belief is not a clear Christian belief. She talks of 'vicarious religion'. In that, she means that most people do not want to go to church but they are very glad that someone does and sees them doing it 'on their behalf'! This situation is unlikely to be with us for long.

But a drop off in belonging does not necessarily mean a fall in believing. Other institutions have found a similar decline in a desire for 'membership' or formal belonging.

If we try and maintain 'business as usual', the church as we know it, will surely die.

Spirituality thriving

G.K. Chesterton is credited with the remark, 'When people stop believing in God, they do not believe in nothing, they believe in anything.'

If we believe that all human beings are by nature spiritual since they are made in the image of God, then they cannot become secularised or de-spiritualised purely by living in a secular environment. They may lose touch with religious belief and systems but their desire for spiritual life will remain.

What is very interesting in Britain is that as church attendance appears to be going down and secularisation increases, spiritual experiences appear to be on the increase.

David Hay, an empirical researcher on the nature of religious or spiritual experience for more than twenty-five years, has done some very interesting research on the spiritual and religious beliefs in Britain. Interested to see whether the decline in church attendance was related to people's understanding and awareness of spiritual experience, Hay compared questions in the BBC's 'Soul of Britain' survey of 2000 with those he had asked in research 13 years earlier. The dramatic increase in positive rates to all his questions took him by surprise.

Here is the summary of his findings:

FREQUENCY OF REPORT OF RELIGIOUS OR SPIRITUAL EXPERIENCE IN BRITAIN FOR YEARS 1987 AND 2000

	1987	2000	% Increase
A patterning of events/transcendent providence	29%	55%	90%
Awareness of the presence of God	27%	38%	41%
Awareness of prayer being answered	25%	37%	48%
Awareness of a sacred presence in nature	16%	29%	81%
Awareness of the presence of the dead	18%	25%	39%
Awareness of an evil presence	12%	25%	108%

Evangelism in a Spiritual Age (Church House Publishing, 2005) quoted from David Hay and Kate Hunt's, *Understanding the Spirituality of People Who Don't Go to Church* (University of Nottingham, 2000)

David Hay and others have come to some important conclusions out of these findings.

- People are more open about their spiritual experiences than before (this may account for some of the increase in experiences).

- The under-forty age group are far less likely to have had some formal religious experience than those over forty. This is born out by recent statistics showing that 40 per cent of the under-forties have never been to church (apart from Christmas, the odd wedding, or similar occasions).

- Everybody's spirituality is unique depending on their life history, background and the cultural context in which they grew up.

- Most people describe themselves as on a journey of discovery.

- The majority believe in 'something out there' as opposed to a well-formed understanding of God.

- Many people live with the contradiction of struggling with 'a God who allows suffering' and the belief in a God who helps them with their personal needs.

- The church is a major barrier to most people and is seen as hypocritical and out of touch with reality. This is often related to a lack of authenticity on behalf of Christians where they are perceived as behaving inconsistently in the work environment.

- The immanence of God is far easier to grasp than his transcendence.
- Many men want to talk about spiritual things but are particularly concerned about how they are viewed by their friends.

Note: Before we get too excited we must underline that this new openness about spirituality does not mean everyone is about to find God. The scene is full of the weird and the wonderful and often very self-gratifying. In fact many people's search for spiritual experience is adamantly opposed to it being linked to religion. They do not want to be committed to anything, but rather experience a place of personal enlightenment and well-being free of the trappings of religious affiliation.

What this does underline is the need to move from speaking to listening. We must first hear a person's journey before we can begin to help them further.

In outlining these findings, we have not intended to deal with any of these issues in a detailed way. Many others have done that and will continue to do so as we get more understanding. The purpose here is purely to show the emergence of a number of streams of change that lead to a considerable amount of turbulence. It is no wonder we feel uneasy and unsure of the way forward.

And there is more!

Society changing

A CONSUMER SOCIETY

Many people now see themselves as consumers not producers. There is a far greater desire to take out rather than put in. Therefore, people's attitude to spirituality, religion and church will reflect that. In their spiritual search, they will look as a consumer as to what fits them best. If they decide to go to church, they will look around for what suits them and not feel any sense of having to stay with one group although brand loyalty is still a factor for many. This means people will look at church as a place where their needs can be met and they will want to know that it fits their style and way of doing things. If not, they will merely shop around.

DISAPPEARING NEIGHBOURHOODS

Most people no longer work and live in the same place, nor are their social relationships found in the geographical area where they live. So the concept of neighbourhood is very different from what it was. There is less commitment to a place. It becomes harder for the church to identify with a specific area, except in some rural areas. Evangelism in the workplace will rarely affect the church in which the Christian belongs. This means that we have to develop both a closer collaboration of churches together ('I realise you cannot come to the Alpha course at my church but we have a branch near you that will help!) and the possibility of work-related 'church' developing.

It is interesting to note that many city and town councils are seeking ways to regenerate local communities and in many cases looking to the church to help. This could be a very creative development for the church in mission.

MOBILE SOCIETY

We are used to travelling to get what we want. We drive to the shops and cinema and travel to meet our friends. We are a society on the move and therefore will have to devise strategies to cater for such mobility. People on the move will have to be reached on the move.

NETWORK RELATIONSHIPS

Our social circle and area of influence will be in the network we have created for ourselves. Work colleagues may be the strongest and closest network we have, or our network might be formed by a common love for a sport or leisure activity. Evangelism will almost always be most effective within the networks we are part of and not necessarily the neighbourhoods we belong to. The local church will need to recognise and take advantage of these networks rather than force people into un-natural circles and relationships. This again may have repercussions for the nature of church. If a network Is to be reached then an expression of church may have to be formed within it, which may look a little different from the norm of church as we know it.

24/7 LIVING

With shops and many workplaces open every day and some all night, things have changed as to how we relate work and leisure. For most people the weekend is still a time off work but flexi working is changing many people's patterns and rhythms of life. The idea that Sunday is the only day to do church would have to be seriously questioned if we are going to both provide for the 'I'm away most weekends' Christian and those whose children play sport on a Sunday morning, or seriously provide for the non-Christian who is thinking seriously about church but for whom Sundays is already unavailable. There is no hour of the day or night or day of the week when the gathering of believers could not take place.

COMMUNICATION REVOLUTION

The revolution brought about by email, the mobile phone and computer technology, have changed the way and the speed with which we can communicate. And it has only just begun. There is absolutely no point in enumerating the latest amazing developments in communication technology because as soon as you grasp it, it has moved on. But if the Roman roads provided a way for the gospel to travel in the first century, how can the new highways be equally used? Surely, vastly improved communication channels must be able to be used to spread the good news. The opportunities are there to be seized.

And it is hard out there!

Don't be in any doubt that this is a difficult time for the church. It is full of uncertainty. It is not a time for the faint hearted or for those looking for a quick fix solution. It is a time to build well and make the changes that will benefit future generations as well as ours. But, at the same time, if you look below the radar you will see signs of hope and life appearing.

It is a time for perseverance, for faithfulness to the gospel, for adventures in faith. When you have nothing to lose then it is a time to be daring and go for it.

Do not despise or throw out the old. Do not be afraid of the new and the untried.

At the end of the day, we are going to need what Eugene Peterson calls, 'A long obedience in the same direction.' (*A Long Obedience in the Same Direction*, InterVarsity Press, 1980)

A TIME TO CHANGE

We are now in a missionary situation again for the first time in ages. The systems that were set up to pastor an at least nominally Christian nation will not, in the main, work for the situation we are now in. Existing churches will need to alter their approach and new churches will have to be started (and in many quarters this is beginning to happen) if this and future generations are to be reached.

It now requires a different approach. This in turn requires the courage of people and leaders to change the way we do things.

If we are willing to question what we do in a constructive way, refocus and take steps of faith, Scripture and history encourages us that there is a 'hope and a future' for those at present living in exile.

The way forward, old or new?

As people begin to search for faith, existing churches will be the place that some will still come to, either in order to find faith or to grow in their faith. These will most probably be people who have had some connection with church in the past. They will remember Christendom and have some understanding of Christianity and feel that church has a sense of 'going home'.

The sorts of church that will be best suited for those 'returning' are as varied as could be imagined. Many younger people are attracted to very traditional, cathedral-style worship services. This is also borne out by the tens of thousands of young people who visit Taize every year and find God in quiet contemplation and reflective worship. Others are drawn to the loud, vibrant and enthusiastic style of other expressions of church. Others are drawn to places with a particular style and emphasis of teaching. So, who knows what is best? That is the joy of variety in the body of Christ. The key is that we have a heart for welcoming in those who are finding God in their lives.

But, there will be many others for who church as we know it is too big a step and culturally on another planet. There are increasing numbers of people who have never been to church and have no experience at all of what church is like. Nor are they interested to find out, but they may feel attracted to Jesus.

If we are serious about reaching them we must start where they are. We will have to be prepared to meet these people half way and not expect them to become like us in our church expression. We may want to provide church for them but it may be expressed in a new way.

Vincent Donavan in his book, *Christianity Rediscovered* (Orbis Books, 2003), writes

> Do not try to call them back to where they were.
> Do not call them to where you are,
> beautiful as that place may seem to you.
>
> You must have the courage to go to a place
> where neither you nor they have ever been before.

There is no suggestion of purely discarding the old as for many, the old is exactly what they need to discover and grow in their faith. But for others it will not be, nor should it.

This promises to be a great adventure even if rather scary.

But the heart of all this is still church even though it may look a little different from what we have known for some time.

Later in this book we have unpacked what we consider to be the three non-negotiable elements of church: mission, spirituality and community. After all, if church means anything, there must be fundamentals that make it church as opposed to anything else. If we can distinguish between the essentials and what has been attached through centuries of Christendom living, we will be less careful to hang on to what we do not need and more prepared to move out into untried territory.

Having set the foundations down, the second half illustrates this with real stories of present day adventures, some of which have been labelled 'fresh expressions of church'.

Fresh expressions of church

All over the place new forms of church are springing forth. They are called by some people, 'emerging church', 'new expressions' of church or just 'church plants'. Many of these will be seen to be 'enthusiasms' which do not last but out of the wide variety some will fully take root and grow. All that is new is not necessarily good but it must at least be heralded as seeking to do the right thing.

What can be observed about them is

THERE IS NO PARTICULAR MODEL

It is impossible to put a frame around them, which is a great strength. Some look very similar to existing churches and are just the same thing planted in a new situation. Some barely look like a church at all but if you look carefully will have the basic fundamentals at their heart.

THERE IS A REAL DESIRE TO BE RADICAL

It is a way of thinking as much as a way of doing. Those involved in new ways of doing church feel an unease with what they have experienced in traditional settings and know they cannot reach their friends that way. Many do not know what it is they are searching for and therefore so much of what they do has a very experimental feel about it. That leaves them vulnerable to criticism when what they need is encouragement. Sadly there are always people wanting them to fail.

MISSION IS THE KEY

Those that start out purely as a reaction to the church they belong to, seeking for a better way to be church, rarely survive. If the goal is to search for church utopia alone, it will as often as not peter out before long. The majority do what they do because they see it as the only way to reach certain groups of people and they claim success only if people find faith.

 A note of caution here: Some people say that the reason they have to begin something new is because 'my friends would never enjoy a normal church.' The question is, 'How do you know? Most people have never been.'

So be careful not to put thoughts and opinions into the minds of non-Christians that they are not thinking. Some non-Christians would not feel at home in the conventional church but a lot would if given the chance. If we genuinely have the not-yet-Christian in mind then we will be sure to find out what is best for them, which may be another church that already exists rather than one that is newly formed.

Kevin Ward quotes Harvey Cox ('Is New Zealand's Future Churchless??' Inaugural Lecture 23/02/2004)

> So far only faint harbingers of the new era are discernable. If the qualities of most of the new religious movements presage anything, we may expect a world that prefers equality to hierarchy, participation to submission, experience over abstraction, multiple rather than single meanings, and plastificity rather than fixedness.

And he continues, commenting about New Zealand, but appropriate in Europe

> If churches do embody these principles, then the forms they take will undergo and process of significant further change. Church leaders could do worse than take the philosophy of Mao Tse Tung's cultural revolution in China and seek to 'let a thousand flowers bloom.' Some will wither and die very quickly, some will doubtless become non-orthodox or heretical, but among those that thrive are likely to be found new social groupings needed to contextualise our faith into the new world of post Christian, postmodern and post secular New Zealand.

22 principles of becoming mission-minded

In this section we are outlining a number of general principles that help a church be mission focused. The church stories in the later part of the book illustrate many of these principles.

Always put principle before method

DRILLS OR HOLES

A well-known manufacturer of electric drills invited, at great expense, a consultant to come and analyse the company and determine why they were no longer keeping up with their competitors. He spent some time in the company and eventually called the board together to give them the benefit of his very costly wisdom. He said, 'I have concluded three simple things:

1. You make drills
2. You do not make drills
3. You make holes.'

That was the conclusion of his lengthy deliberations! After the initial shock had died down and the anger at the apparent stupidity of his conclusions had abated, they began to take in what he was saying and it changed the whole course of the company. They focused on making holes and developed a whole new technology with lasers.

The leadership of the company had been focusing on a model, in this case the electric drill. They needed to look at the principle and in this case the need of people to be able to make holes.

Principle: We do not do church, we make disciples

Church is a means of disciple making. Everything we do should be centred around what we are actually called to do. The principle behind all Christian ministry should be that we are called to worship God and to make disciples.

If we are called to make disciples, then how are we to go about it? Again it begins with principles.

'OFF THE SHELF MODELS' WILL NOT WORK

The Christian church, in its desire to be effective, all too readily grabs models off the shelf assuming that if it works for 'them' it will work for us. The only reason that it works for 'them' is because at some stage they looked at the principle and sought to apply that principle in a way that suited their present situation.

If, as we mentioned earlier, Europe is 'an exceptional case', then it is unlikely that methods that work in another culture will automatically work here. But the principle on which the method is based may be very valid and can be reworked in other contexts.

Although it is important not to always have to 're-invent the wheel', God will uniquely and creatively shape what is right for each particular place at a particular time.

This principle applies too from one country to another in Europe or even from one town to another.

- For example, when the team from **Willow Creek Community Church** first came to Britain, they caused a lot of excitement with their passion and ways of reaching people, and many of us were quick to read their message as 'seeker services are the key'. Actually the principle they were trying to communicate was 'prioritise unchurched people and learn to speak their language in order to reach them.' And then, 'Oh, by the way, this is what we do.' It was all too easy to be caught up with 'what we do' as opposed to 'why we do it.'

- **Alpha** is another example of this. Everybody can see that Alpha (and other similar courses) is having a huge impact and is very effective in what it is attempting to do. Probably, the place it is most effective is Holy Trinity Brompton. Why? Because for them it was not an off the shelf model, it came out of understanding a principle. On what principles does Alpha work and succeed?

     The answer is four things.

     1. *Friendship* is the best way for people to hear about Jesus.

     2. *Food* is a huge help in making people feel at home and eating is something we all have in common with everyone.

     3. *A non-Sunday* event is much easier for the 'interested but not committed' person to come to. (*Charles Spurgeon wrote of his observation that more non-believers would come and hear him preach on a Thursday than a Sunday. His conclusion was that if they came on a Sunday they were making two commitments; one to hear about Jesus, the other to come to church. Most were ready and willing for the one but not the other. So they came on Thursday.*)

     4. People need *time to process* the gospel in their lives.

In other words if the four principles mentioned are true, you must shape what you do around them and not the model. Anything that encompassed those principles would be effective to some degree.

A young lady was cooking bacon in the frying pan and before she started she cut off both ends. When asked why, she said it was because her mother always did. When she asked her mother why she did it, she said she didn't know but it was because her mother did. Fortunately, grandmother was still alive so they asked her why she cut the bacon at both ends. 'Oh,' she said, 'when I was young the pan we had was so very small, the long pieces of bacon that we used to buy wouldn't fit in the pan so we always cut it at both ends to make it fit!'

The model had been passed down but nobody stopped to ask what the principle was on which it was based.

There are a number of courses around today that are working well because they are based on the same principles. There are some places that are struggling with Alpha because they are trying to do exactly as HTB do without looking at the cultural differences between the two.

The point here is not to debate Alpha but to underline the importance of principle over model or method. It is all too easy (and expensive) to chase round the world looking at success stories and trying to copy what they do. There may be a principle that they have got hold of that you have neglected but do not confuse it with the method they have used or expect that to be a model for you.

There are many wrong assumptions being made. If you see a successful work and examine the methods they use, you could think that the method caused the success. The other possibility is that it channelled success. In other words the growth forced the structure to emerge; the structure did not cause the growth. The structure was not the cause but the effect. So, if you copy it you will end up with an empty vessel. It won't produce for you because it did not in fact produce for them. The Methodist cell system did not produce revival. It channelled it.

MODELS CAN DISCOURAGE

Many models can leave you unbelievably discouraged! You may go and visit some great church and come away impressed, overawed and full of enthusiasm. Then you return to the reality of Morton in the Mud parish church and you are filled with discouragement and despair. If you are hounded by the thoughts that if only you could have their success and their facilities, life would be good, you might have been better off staying at home and never travelling! But if you came away with one or two simple principles your visit would have been worthwhile.

In the next few pages we are going to talk about a number of key principles for church life that will be true whoever and wherever you are.

CAN WE LEARN FROM BUSINESS?

The church is primarily a family not a business but the answer is yes and no. Yes, in that we are talking about helping a group of people move in a particular direction. No, if the bottom line is profit not people.

In his excellent and well-researched book, *Good to Great* (Random House, 2001), Jim Collins describes the characteristics of companies that in his mind moved from being good companies to being great companies. There are some interesting parallels between what he discovered for companies and what would be true for the church. These are interwoven into some of the principles that follow. We are surrounded today by what people describe as good churches. They are the fruit of years of both renewal within the mainstream church, and the development of new churches. But things are changing and these churches will have to move on to greatness or in time they will lose the plot and begin the downward slope to ineffectiveness and could disappear altogether.

In this fast changing environment, it is no longer an option for us to stay as we are. Good is not good enough.

In defining greatness, it would be easy to assume that it meant size and influence but we would want to challenge that strongly. *Greatness in this context is a measure of health and not size*. We are all aware that something that grows is not necessarily healthy. Health means that everything is doing what it is meant to do. There are all sorts of flowers in my garden. I do not want them all large or all small but I do want them to be healthy.

We define greatness in terms of health, i.e. a healthy church is one that is doing what it was meant to do.

What the church is meant to be doing is continuing the incarnation. Jesus was God incarnate. He fully expressed the life of God in a human life. The church as the body of Christ is called to express the life and ministry of Jesus to the present culture in a way that it can understand and to which it can respond. It is on this assumption of incarnation that everything else that follows will be built.

Remember: Methods often change. Principles never do.

Questions you might ask

- On what principles is our church based?

- What methods have we taken 'off the shelf?'

- What were the underlying principles in these areas?

- What are we doing that is not principle based?

Ask questions.
Do not hurry to the answers

'You have never been this way before,' was Joshua's word to the people as they prepared to enter the unchartered territory of the Promised Land (Josh. 3:4, NIV). When faced with a totally new situation, you tend not to have too many answers right away, but if you don't ask questions you will never make it. At the end of each section we ask questions that provoke us all to be real and honest about where we are at and where we want to go. This is a very different world from the one our parents and grand parents knew. It is very disorientating but there must be a way through and when we find it, it will be fruitful as it was for the children of Israel.

If you have ever had any experience of life-coaching you will know that the key is to have someone ask you questions without giving you answers. You find the answers for yourself and are then held accountable by your coach for the steps you take.

The answer is closer than you think.

Reading other people's experience and wisdom can be helpful and inspiring, but we don't just need lots of books of answers. If we ask the questions the answers may well be close at hand. The trouble is that the answer might involve considerable cost.

If you are leader, you and your team should always be asking searching questions. If you are not a leader, don't be afraid to ask your leaders the important questions.

When I go on a journey I like to ask, 'Where are we going? How are going to get there? What will it cost? When do we leave and arrive? Why are we making this journey? Which clothes should I take?

If we are to be effective in the present climate, almost everything we do should be up for grabs. We are all carrying clutter and we may have to shed much of if we are to be prepared for the future. When you leave home on a journey you cannot take everything with you (even though many of us try). In fact, apart from three fundamentals of church that are described more fully later, everything is potentially expendable. If we are to turn the church into a mission station, we better do a thorough inventory of what we are doing and why we are doing it and then put it up against what we now want to achieve.

One popular writer on leadership in the business world said that a great leader doesn't have to produce all the answers and then try to motivate others to follow his (or her) vision. However it does mean they must have the humility to see that they do not yet understand enough to have the answers, but be willing to ask questions that will then lead on to the best insights.

In your present situation, ask yourselves questions about why you do what you do, how fruitful you are being, what is worth keeping and what should stop. Don't be afraid of questions and do not be surprised if you do not have quick or easy answers. But questions are the first step to answers.

Questions you might ask

- What are the key questions your leaders are wrestling with?

- What steps are you taking to hear people's concerns?

- How much time do you spend listening to others?

Start with mission. Church will follow

There has been much debate over the last few years about the shape and nature of the future church. Nobody really knows what it will look like but that has not prevented all sorts of ideas being put forward. There are those who are tired with church as it is and set out to produce church on their ideal lines. The idea being that if we get church right everything else will follow.

Others are starting new churches spawned off from old, but again often in an attempt to produce, 'what church is really meant to be'.

This way round you end up with church as you want it and then have to ask the question, 'How do we reach out from here?'

This is like a fisherman who finds some worms and asks, 'What sort of fish can I catch with this?' He would be better to ask, 'What do I want to catch? What bait do I need for the job?' and then to go from there.

We are people under orders. Those orders have never been withdrawn in 2,000 years. Jesus' last instructions were to 'make disciples'. There are no instructions in the New Testament to build or plant churches. Church came out of mission. In other words, church is the result of mission not the other way round. The church of the future will be the shape which is both the result of mission and the shape that causes it best to happen. But its form will be dictated by the nature of doing mission in the twenty-first century.

The first church after the day of Pentecost was formed as a result of mission. The churches that arose following the dispersion of Acts 8 came as result of them going everywhere preaching the gospel. The churches across Asia Minor came from Paul and his team finding ways to bring people to Jesus in a cross-cultural context. Church was what you got when you had brought people to Christ and found a way to bring them into community so that they could grow as disciples.

These early Christians wrestled with the questions of mission before they ever worked out church. We are in a missionary period of our history. We have to learn all over again. We are more likely to get it right if we get it in the right order.

 Key: You must start with mission. Let the shape or reshaping of church follow.

Again, you start by asking questions.

Questions you might ask

- Who are we trying to reach? Which group of people are we best equipped to influence with the gospel?

- The answer to that question will almost certainly relate to the cultural make-up of the existing group of believers who have a heart for mission. The likelihood is that there will already be a bridge into this community. It may, for example, be age, life stage, sports, or work-related. Find the existing links.

In some cases people may feel called by God to move across cultures into a people group where there is no obvious point of contact but even here, points of contact must be found by serving that particular group in a way that gives you a voice. This invariably takes time and patience.

- What are the specific points of need in this group of people?

- What are the needs in our community? What can we do to serve them?

- How can we best introduce them to Jesus through serving?

Then you might ask the questions

- What will best enable these people to grow?

- What structure would best express church for them?

- Would they easily fit into an already existing church or would it be best to start something new amongst that group of people?

And only then you might ask the questions

- When should we meet?

- Where should we meet?

- How should we meet?

- What will allow these folk to experience church life that both helps believers and also acts as a mission to others?

In other words, provided we have the basic ingredients of church (mission, community and spirituality) the shape can be infinitely flexible to best suit the culture of the people we are reaching.

Remember this is applicable to those starting new expressions of church as well as those starting a new congregation within an existing church structure. If you are reaching young families with kids who play football on Sunday morning, you don't disciple them by making them turn out at 10.30 a.m. every Sunday . . . you find a time that suits them.

Church planting only needs to happen if the situation demands it because a particular group of people cannot be reached or discipled any other way.

In the past we have made the mistake that we must 'church plant at all costs'. Actually we must share the good news at all costs and plant if necessary.

 Note: George Whitfield admitted at the end of his life that he had not been as wise as John Wesley. He had left no structure to disciple new converts.

Both had prioritised mission in their lives but only the latter had sought to build church as a fruit of it. In fact the Methodist class system was devised to enable new converts to be discipled and then grow in their faith within a community. The Methodist churches grew out of mission.

Questions you might ask

- Are we asking the right questions?!

- What is the single biggest unanswered question for us at the present time?

- Are we deciding on church questions ahead of mission questions?

- What people group or groups are we seeking to reach and what church structure will best suit them?

- Who in our congregation is ready and prepared to pioneer something new?

The church has to turn inside out

The following statistics have been well circulated. At the present time in the UK it is estimated that approximately (these are rounded figures but the first is actually now closer to 8 per cent)

10 per cent attend church regularly (monthly)

10 per cent attend church occasionally

20 per cent have left church for negative reasons

20 per cent have left the church by drifting away

40 per cent have never been to church.

(Stats: Francis and Richter, *Gone but not forgotten*, Darton, Longman & Todd, 1998)

CONSIDER THE 40 PER CENT

The 40 per cent figure is increasing in the under-forties every year. This group of people will have never been to church, and they will have less Bible knowledge and less understanding of even the basics of Christian faith. It is not totally insignificant that the questions concerning the Bible in the TV show *Who Wants to be a Millionaire?* come quite late in the game and are considered difficult questions; a question concerned the shortest book in the Old Testament and it was for £500,000! The assumption is that most people have very little Bible knowledge, which is increasingly the case.

NEUTRAL GROUND

Because church is not in the frame of their thinking, even at a time of spiritual searching they are very unlikely to seek a church out for help. The spiritual search may not be a search for religion. They will not associate a spiritual need with a religious answer. Therefore to assume that they will make their way into church is both naïve and unkind. They will not come home because they never left – it never was home.

Therefore if they won't be coming to church to satisfy their search, there is only one way they will hear and that is by someone going to them.

TIME. LOTS OF IT

Not only will they not be coming to church, they will need time to understand the gospel. People without a foundation need to receive understanding in order to make a response. Understanding, when you know nothing, takes time. That is why courses such as 'Alpha' and 'Discovering Christianity' are such a help. But even these are short and many people find they have to do them twice to begin to get hold of what it is about.

They will only get understanding if someone goes to them and offers an ongoing means of giving them understanding.

A CLEAR EXAMPLE

Thirdly, most people in this category really do not know what a Christian actually is. They may have negative ideas based on perceptions gained from scandals, soaps or public figures. They may need to see a consistent Christian life lived out in front of them, before they will begin to take a look. They can only do that in an out of church experience.

> It will be the consistent theme of these pages that the hope for the future lies in an inside out church. What is at present an outside in church must have a major turn around to become inside out!

IT HAS HAPPENED BEFORE

If we are looking for a biblical parallel, then seeing how the early church reached the Gentiles is not far off. The Jews had a religious framework to their lives; they knew the Old Testament. So the gospel was preached initially to people who had a foundation of understanding. But not so the Gentile world.

When Paul went to Ephesus (Acts 19), he found a mix of people, some Jews and mostly non-Jews. He started preaching to the Jews in the synagogue and persisted for three months. When he could get no further with them he moved out and he went to a neutral place, the hall of Tyrannus. It was easily accessible for Jews and Greeks alike. He did not ask the Greeks to come into the alien environment of a synagogue. He went to a place that was easy for them to go to. The advantage of neutral ground was that it was easy for the non-Jews but also accessible to the Jews.

EVERY DAY FOR TWO YEARS!

Then he stayed there, preaching every day for two years. Two years! People would have come time and time again to build up their knowledge and understanding of the Christian faith. He realised that without background knowledge they needed to have time to understand what it was all about. Then they needed time to grow in their faith.

The fact that Luke was able to say that, 'all the Jews and Greeks who lived in the province of Asia heard the word of the Lord' (Acts 19:10, NIV) is extraordinary. What he quite meant we don't know but obviously the influence was very extensive

If we are going to communicate the good news to an ever-increasing number of the population who have no church background, most of whom are not antagonistic to Jesus, we must go where they are and we must meet them on their ground. And it will take time – possibly a lot of time.

This is one of the main keys for unlocking the future. It sounds obvious but *the mindset of the western Christian is almost the opposite*.

For more on this look at the section on 'the scattered church', in the section on 'Mission' later in the book, pages 85–87.

Questions you might ask

- How much of our thinking is geared to the 40 per cent unchurched?

- Do we have any strategy for reaching this group?

- On a scale of one to ten, how focused are the church members on those outside the church?

- How do we plan to refocus them?

- How will we know when it has happened?

Put non-Christian people high on the agenda

Up to this point, most of what we do in church life is concerned with nurturing, feeding, helping, and teaching Christians. The resources we have from money given, the time of those in full-time work, and the spare time of the church members primarily goes to keeping the ship afloat.

The checks we put on ourselves will tend to be about whether the offerings are enough, how good the service was, what the worship was like this week, who is unhappy with us at the moment, and do we have enough people to run children's church. All well and good but hardly enough to change the world.

A fundamental principle of mission church is that *the people we think about most are those not yet in the kingdom*. Of course we must care for the people in the church, and of course we want good services but the yardstick must be our effect on the unbeliever. The nature of being a church in mission is that everyone from the person who serves coffee to the preacher, is concerned about unbelievers and the effect they are having on them.

A mission church is also one in which every department of the church's life, whether it be children's work, men's ministry or the elderly, *has the reaching of non-Christian people at the heart of their thinking and planning.*

The truth is that at present the average believer doesn't care very much provided their needs are being met. We have lived for so long in maintenance mode that we have forgotten who really matters. This will require a complete mindset change for leaders and people alike.

If Jesus is to be our example and surely he must be, since he said, 'As the Father has sent me, I am sending you' (Jn. 20:21, NIV), then we must follow his pattern which was both to help, encourage and release 12 men into mission, and to give his attention to ordinary people in need. This means both developing and nurturing new Christians as well as reaching new people for Christ.

The only way to do this effectively is by always trying to see things through the eyes of the unbeliever. They are rarely antagonistic eyes, it is just that they do not understand. *It is important to ask how they see things, what is important to them and ultimately what is best for them.*

For many of us who have been Christians for a long time, that may be difficult. If the default mode for us as Christians tends towards the religious, we will have to work hard to change our way of thinking.

 Remember the story of the good shepherd. The shepherd left the 99 to go after the one! What does that say about priorities?

Questions you might ask

- Looking at you church programme, how much is giving priority to unchurched people?

- What would it mean to you to prioritise those outside?

- In what areas would you need to make some changes?

- What do you plan to do about it?

Church is people not buildings

If we are going to return to the flexibility and mobility of both the early church and other very effective times of mission in Europe, such as the Celtic movement, we are going to have to get our eyes off buildings as a prerequisite to successful church. At the end of the day, a building is a place to meet in to keep out of the rain! (Although, it is true to say that if the meeting place is too small it will restrict growth.)

When most people talk about church they are referring to a building and not a community of people. In the first few centuries, the 'church' was always known as a group of people; where they met was secondary.

So much time, money and energy is put into buildings that they can so easily become a distraction to mission. We need places to meet but they must serve the primary purpose to help us reach people for Christ.

The expression, 'go to church' underlines the problem. We need to be re-educated to realise that we do not 'go' to church, we 'belong' to church. The question, 'which church do you belong to?' is better than, 'where do you go to church?'

The church to which Nick belongs in Birmingham is called Riverside. The name has nothing to do with a physical river but relates to an understanding of church based on Ezekiel 47. In that picture the river of God flows from the temple. It flows out into the dry and barren area bringing life wherever it goes. Church is the people of God, filled with his Spirit going out into the barren areas of society bringing life. It is not a river flowing into a building but from it.

Why spend money on a building if you do not have to? Many of them are used for one day a week. *If you decide to build, do so in such a way that it serves the community seven days a week and does not isolate the real church*. It is also important that whatever building we do use makes people feel comfortable and at ease. The building must serve the primary focus of our life at this time and that is mission. We are no longer settlers. We are a people on the move and must liberate ourselves from the old mentality in order to become pioneers all over again.

> What the early Church did not have were buildings — for nearly three hundred years! That is why at Saddleback church we waited until we had over ten thousand in attendance before we built our first building. We wanted to prove that the church is people, not a building. If you want to be truly vintage church, don't build a building!
>
> Rick Warren (quoted in Dan Kimball, *The Emerging Church*, Zondervan 2003)

A pastor of a large church in the USA was lecturing at a college. When he finished speaking, he asked for questions. The first question was, 'I have visited your city on many occasions but never been to your church. Could you tell us exactly where it is?'

He thought for a moment and replied, 'I really do not know, I am afraid!' This was received with disbelief. He went on to say, 'Well let me have a go at answering it. Mary, who is a nurse is in the hospital. Bill is probably driving the no.17 bus. John is a lawyer and so is most likely in his office.' He paused. 'Is that enough or do you want to know more?'

Then he continued, 'You probably want to know where the building is that we meet in. Well, you should have asked! You actually asked me where the church was.'

Questions you might ask

- How much of our time and energy is building focused?
- What could we do outside our own building?
- What percentage of budget is for the building and what for ministry?
- Is our present building causing a restriction on growth?
- If so, what are we going to do about it?

You cannot achieve anything without purpose

It is absolutely vital that you know why you exist as a church and to have some idea where you are going. You may not be sure at all of what the final outcome will look like but you must set a course. It is surprising that many churches do not seem to know why they are there or where they are going. It is very helpful to write things down in order to make it clear for ourselves. Almost certainly you will not know what the end point will look like but it will at least give you something to aim for. The following is important for a new venture or redefining the old.

PURPOSE: WHAT ARE WE HERE FOR?

It is incredibly important to have some form of purpose or mission statement. The very act of working it through can revolutionise what you do and how you prioritise. It needs to be *easy to remember* so that everyone involved can, almost without hesitation, express the church's purpose. Then everything else you do can be measured up against it. If what you are currently doing does not fit the purpose, then you can get rid of it. It may be good but it will slow you down in the main thing you are seeking to achieve.

  It must express reality, not be meaningless!

VALUES: WHAT IS IMPORTANT TO US?

Every group or church has values. It is helpful to write these down so that again you can make sure that what you do is aligned with them. Values are often not things you make up, they are what you observe about yourselves and the way you do things.

VISION: WHERE ARE WE GOING?

It is helpful to say where you'd like to be in a year/five years' time. What are you seeking to achieve? It might be a new congregation, impact on a housing estate, an outreach to young mums, or any other such thing.

  Note: You will overestimate what you can achieve in one year. You will almost certainly underestimate what you can achieve in five years!

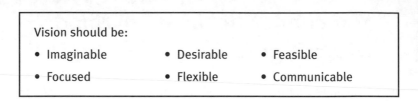

Vision should be:

- Imaginable   - Desirable   - Feasible
- Focused   - Flexible   - Communicable

STRATEGY: HOW WILL WE GET THERE?

Every new idea needs some plans to make it work. We may all decide we want to achieve something but we need to know how we might get there. There are quite a lot of places with mission statements and they sound great. They trip off the tongue but actually lack reality. Reality is shown up when you think about strategy. The thing that will test every mission statement is to ask the key question, 'OK, so that is what we say we'd like to do, but how on earth are we going to do it?'

GOALS: WHAT WILL WE DO AND BY WHEN?

This takes it even further.

Goals help us to make a start. Goals are the only things that are totally dependent on us. Either we fulfil them or we don't. We can hold each other and ourselves accountable for goals.

We would suggest that all churches wanting to be effective in mission, write down their purpose, values, vision, strategy and goals. The latter two will change as you go along.

These all help us to chart a course. Along the way, God may redirect us and refine things but at least we set the sails and launch out. Who knows, we might even catch the wind?

Questions you might ask

- If asked, would every member of the church know our mission/purpose statement?
- Do we know what it is?
- Is it in practice the plumb line of church policy?
- What is our vision and what strategy do we have for reaching it?
- Can we answer these questions easily or do they expose a lack of clarity?
- What are we going to do about it?

The Holy Spirit is working in the world

This sounds obvious but it isn't at all. In fact, the mindset of most of us as Christians is quite the reverse. The way we act, the things we say, the songs we sing in the main demonstrate that we believe the exclusive work of the Spirit is in the church. Of course, it is true that if we have opened ourselves to him, the Holy Spirit takes up residence in us. We are the temple of the Holy Spirit both individually and corporately. But it would be quite wrong to limit him to this alone.

Most of us, if we search our hearts, would be able to testify to the fact that long before we came to Christ, we had a sense of 'being pursued'. We may not have put it like that at the time, but when we look back we can see how God was gently speaking to us. Our conversion was the end of a process.

Mission becomes so much more exciting when you work on this principle. *The principle is that God loves people more than you do and he is already influencing their lives*. But He needs our help for them to find him.

In fact, it has been said that every culture already has a redemption story that needs only to be explained and interpreted. This is almost certainly true of individuals as well.

The assumption that the Holy Spirit is at work outside the church as well as within it, is absolutely fundamental to mission in a post-Christendom society.

Remember Daniel! He found himself living and working in an alien but spiritually diverse culture. He was far away from his natural Jewish surroundings, having the support of a few very close friends who helped one another remain faithful to God. The story recounts that God spoke to the king before Daniel ever had a chance to.

Nebuchadnezzar had a God-inspired dream that he did not understand. He already believed in the supernatural having surrounded himself with magicians and enchanters to help him. But here they could not help and, as we know, Daniel knew someone who could, the Living God.

What was his role? To listen and to interpret what was happening.

Remember Peter! He seriously struggled with the possibility that God could really have any time for Gentiles. And then he made an amazing discovery; Cornelius, a man from a Gentile background who was open to God, received a vision from God. He was obviously a man who longed for God but had no idea how to reach him. Peter realised that God was speaking to Cornelius before he himself ever got to speak to him.

What was Peter's role? To listen and to interpret what was happening.

Could it be that in an increasingly alien world, God is already speaking to spiritually sensitive people? They don't want church or organised religion (certainly not at this point) but they are on a spiritual quest.

And God is already at work. Those who work amongst Muslims and those of other faiths will testify to the considerable number receiving visions and having dreams of a spiritual nature. It must be true of all races of people because God loves them and he rewards those who seek after him.

What is our role? To listen and to interpret what is happening.

 Remember. Evangelism begins with listening and seeking to understand another person's spiritual journey. It is a process as they discover the God who is speaking to them.

We are there to help them in their journey not to tell them they are wrong and demand they believe what we believe. They are likely to get there if we journey with them.

Daniel and Peter both brought understanding to the men they encountered. Both responded to God's intervention in their lives.

It certainly makes life more interesting if you start with the principle that God is already at work.

Questions you might ask

- How do you encourage people to take advantage of this principle?

- What example have you seen from you own life?

- How do you prepare the people for this reality?

- How do you receive feedback as to what they are experiencing among their friends?

There is huge potential in the scattered church

If there is a key to the future this is it. If 40 per cent (and rising by the day) of the public have never been to church, then as already stated, the chances are very small that they are just going to turn up. They will not return to a place they have never been.

Therefore in post Christendom, the church must go to the people. But here is the good news. The church is already among the people! Here is the bad news. The church does not see it!

We have believed for so long that church is what you do when you meet not when you scatter.

> Matthew 28:19 is normally translated, 'Go and make disciples of all nations.'

> What it should read is, 'As you go, make disciples of all nations.' The only command is to 'make disciples'. 'Go' is a present participle, meaning 'going'.

There is a huge difference. The first implies you are in the wrong place even if you are doing the right thing. The second implies you are in the right place but may not be doing the right thing.

Imagine how God views Monday. He sees into the hearts of men and women. Most have rejected church but are spiritually hungry. Their lives are full of need. Inwardly they cry out for help but do not know where to turn. Their heart cry goes to God. They are not going to go to church for help. But on Monday, the church scatters all over the community and lo and behold there is someone close to the person in need. God loves people and he loves to bring the person in need alongside the person with the answer of help. For God and his kingdom, Monday affords a huge opportunity.

Imagine how most Christians view Monday. 'Oh, no, it's Monday again. A whole week of work! Same people. Same job. Sunday service was great. I can't wait for next week and thank goodness for home group on Wednesday. I wish I was in full-time Christian work. I could do so much for God!'

But, every believer is a full-time Christian worker!

If Christians are to be church to the community, we must

1. SEE OURSELVES IN A NEW LIGHT

- I am a missionary sent out from my church into the world of people God has placed me among
- I am filled with the Holy Spirit
- I am a lover of people
- I am a listener and watcher, seeing what God is already doing
- I have a story to tell
- I am a seeker looking for lost people

 Note: Believers must become seekers and signposts. Unbelievers are not seekers. They are people who do not know the way home.

2. SEE OTHERS IN A NEW LIGHT

- People around me are in need
- They do not have the answers to real needs
- They are spiritually hungry
- They have little time for church but may never have heard about Jesus
- They will respond to prayer without antagonism

3. SEE THE CHURCH GATHERING IN A NEW LIGHT

- A place of equipping for life out there
- A place of refreshing
- A place of sending
- A place of welcome to the outsider
- A place of healing for broken people

4. SEE MONDAY IN A NEW LIGHT

- It is the beginning of my week on the mission field where I live out my life as a follower of Jesus and I am looking for people to love.

Above the door in one church where everyone leaving could read it, was a large sign that read, 'WELCOME TO THE MISSION FIELD'.

The scattered church will be

INCARNATIONAL

Incarnation implies the ability to live the Jesus life every day in the company of those we work and live amongst. It demands a consistency between what we say we believe and what we do. It requires us to see no dividing wall between the sacred of church and the secular of work.

It requires the church leaders to be continually teaching and talking about the issues of being a Christian at work. It requires believers to bring all their Christian values to the other areas of their lives.

INSPIRATIONAL

Inspirational is how we live as people empowered by the Holy Spirit. Spiritual men and women are looking for spiritual reality. People are less and less impressed by argument and words alone. They need to experience the power and the love of God for themselves.

At the time of the Exile, Daniel, living in an alien culture, made an impact on the rulers of his day because he was able to interpret dreams and visions. People today are experiencing God through dreams, visions and all sorts of ways. They are looking for explanation. There has probably never been a time of greater openness towards prayer. Almost without exception, men and women today will welcome prayer. What a great opportunity in the workplace, etc. to offer to pray for the needs of our friends and colleagues. When God answers they are on the way to meeting him.

When Jesus used the gifts of the Spirit it was in the 'market place'. The woman at the well had her life changed because Jesus 'knew' all about her. If ever there was a time for the gifts of the Spirit to be relevant it must be now. How great that we know a 'God . . . who reveals mysteries' (Dan. 2:28, NIV).

INVITATIONAL

In a recent survey in the UK, people were asked the question, 'Would you come to a Christian event if someone asked you?'

Eighty per cent said they would! Now they might not have been totally honest but that is a lot of people.

The same number of Christians were asked, 'Do you feel comfortable inviting your non Christian friends to an event?'

Eighty per cent said they would NOT feel comfortable about doing that.

If those figures are anywhere near accurate (especially as the source is unknown) and you want to make an impact, then what would you train believers to do?

It is obvious. Encourage the church to be a crowd of persistent inviters. And make sure you have quality things for them to come to.

The impact could be huge but the word on the street is that 'nobody wants to come'.

In the section on the church as mission, we give some suggestions as to how leaders might encourage this understanding amongst church members.

Questions you might ask

- What are we doing that shows that we believe in the importance of Monday to Friday ministry of the people?

- Do the church see themselves as missionaries?

- How are we going to enable people to see themselves differently?

- What changes will we need to make to release people more fully?

- What spiritual gifts could we use in our 'market place'?

Church gathered can be any time, any place

A fundamental question for us is whether Sunday has to be the day and morning has to be the time for church.

SATURDAY TO SUNDAY

The early church has already demonstrated to us that a change is possible. For them as Jews, the Sabbath, Saturday, was the day set aside as special. They decided to change their day of meeting to Sunday even though this was a working day for most people, the equivalent of Monday to us. They did so because they wanted to celebrate on the first day of the week; the day that Jesus rose from the dead.

There is no reason to change 2,000 years of Christian tradition for the sake of it. It is still vital for everyone to have a Sabbath break (whatever day that might be) and it is still a great idea to celebrate the resurrection at the start of every week.

But in a mission situation, in order to introduce people to the idea of church, we will have to be prepared to gather as church on different days. If church is not a building you go to but a community you belong to, then when and how that meets can have no boundaries. After all, most people who belong to a home group (a very real part of church) usually do so on a weekday. You could easily have small group on Sunday and celebration on Wednesday if it worked better for you.

 Mission church must think outside the Sunday box.

CHOOSE THE TIME

The issue of time is another variable factor. If you continue to meet on a Sunday, it makes sense to find a time (or times) that is most suitable for as many people as possible. There are 24 hours in the day and any time should be a possibility although the middle of the night is unlikely to be popular! If you have sufficient people, then a variety of times might be preferable.

 Mission church must think outside the 11.00 a.m. /6.30 p.m. box.

MISSION MODE REQUIRES FLEXIBILITY

If we were in Christendom mode, a slight alteration might be all that is required. But we are not. We are in mission mode. So for those 'coming back to church' we must ask when is the best time and place for them?

And how about the 'never been to church' crowd who have heard about Jesus through a work colleague and are now making moves toward church of some kind? For many reasons they may not feel Sunday is the best day for them or their family. So why should they be forced into a Sunday mould? Remember, they are joining a family not just coming to a meeting. Surely the important thing is that they come to Christ and they are part of a form of church that enables them to grow and be connected into the wider family of God.

☞ *Mission church must be flexible.*

START WITH THE QUESTION

So what is the answer? That doesn't matter as much as asking the questions. If we will not let go the sacred cow of 'Sunday at 11.00 a.m. and 6.30 p.m.' we have little hope of seeking, finding and bringing home lost sheep. If we do, all sorts of exciting possibilities open up. One church we know of only has one service each Sunday and it is at 4.30 p.m. Another has started a Friday night service for young adults. Others have services midweek. All work very well for those people and their searching friends. If you are cell or congregation based, it becomes even easier to be flexible.

☞ *Mission church must be asking questions.*

Questions you might ask

- Why do we gather when and where we do?

- How long ago were these patterns set down?

- If we could start again with a clean sheet of day/time/place, what would we do?

- Is what you do helpful for those rediscovering church?

- Is it helpful for those with no background in church?

- What would we now need to do to make the changes and what would be the obstacles?

Make returning people welcome

There are many who are coming to faith in Christ today through the witness of friends, or some through courses such as 'Alpha' and the 'Y Course', and are joining churches. Most, but not all, of these will be people who already have some Christian understanding. *They are a part of the de-churched*. Either they were once believers but wandered away, children of Christian parents who rejected their parents' faith or they had some vague contact when they were younger but had chosen to go their own way. This is not exclusively the case but mainly so. Those people naturally lean toward church when they are looking for something. For them it is a sort of coming back because they have a memory. But their view of church is often based on the very distant memory of childhood, their occasional experience through Christmas, weddings, and so on and/or what they have seen on television.

Some who start coming to church may be completely unchurched. For them, it is a complete unknown.

If we really are interested in mission and want people to come into the church, we will need to work hard to make them feel at home.

In the section under 'mission' we have given some pointers to this. Here we are making the point of principle. Every place has to work it out for themselves. But it begins by saying we want to make it easy for people to re-engage with church.

ILLUSTRATION: TRY THE BETTING OFFICE

One Anglican leader recounts his experience of being asked by a man he was trying to befriend, to go into the betting office for him to pick up his winnings. He recalled how that proved to be a most unnerving experience since he was totally outside his comfort zone and felt in a completely alien culture for those few moments. It would not do any of us any harm to find a place that would make us feel the same degree of strangeness and put ourselves deliberately in it. It helps to at least get some sense of empathy with the person coming to a service for the first time.

ILLUSTRATION: HOW ABOUT YOUR OWN HOME?

If you and your family invite someone round for a meal, when you hear the knock on the door you answer it. Your visitors are on the doorstep and you invite them in. I imagine that from then on you would be anxious to make sure they feel at home. You will have your family way of doing things and you cannot change that but at least you would not want your visitors to feel awkward.

If, on the other hand, you just called out, 'the door's open, come on in, make yourselves at home!', and then carried on as if they were not there, they would not feel very welcome. If you then went on watching the TV, your children rushed around the house and you said nothing more to make them feel at home, if you then carried on to eat the meal but never invited them to the table or showed them where to sit, on the basis that 'they ought to know what to do', you would be deemed very rude. I doubt they would stay long. If you treat people coming to your home like that, you will not get many visitors!

If we assume everyone who comes to church 'ought to know what to do' we should not be surprised if they do not stay long.

Questions you might ask

- If a complete stranger came into church, would they feel welcome?

- How do we know?

- If a person were returning after a long break, would they feel welcomed?

- What changes have we made to make outsiders welcome?

- How do we regulate what is going on?

You have to stop before you can start

All transition and all change starts with an ending. You cannot move in a new direction before stopping going in the old one.

If you are fully loaded, you can't pick something up without putting something down.

If you are fully occupied, you cannot do something else if you don't stop doing what you are presently doing.

If the church is to refocus its attention and do things differently, or develop something new in order to be more effective in mission, it cannot do so without making hard choices to stop some things. It is very hard to let good things go for better things, especially if they are uncertain, but many times they don't come into focus until we do exactly that. It takes courage.

William Bridges in his book on *Managing Transitions*, describes three phases that we all have to go through

1. **The Ending.** This is the phase of letting go the old ways and identities of facing losses and coming to terms with the fact that things will not be the same.

   When you have your first baby, you let go of your freedom and independence. It is loss.

   When you change job you let go of many familiar patterns of life.

   It is loss.

   When your children leave home you have to let them go.

   It is a loss.

   When you make changes in order to reach out to unbelievers in a fresh way, you will make changes that will be felt as loss. Own it. Identify it. Grieve it and move on.

2. **The Neutral Zone**. In this period, you have ideas about the new direction but do not know how it will work. It might work out in the way you think or it may turn out different. You feel very vulnerable. People are watching to see if it works or not. You feel a bit at sea.

3. **The New Beginning.** In this phase, everyone finds new energy as they set out on a fresh adventure. When you start a new service, a new form of church, a new ministry, a new expression of the church's life in the community, there's always a buzz around. You realise it was worth the pain of loss in order to break new ground

THE THREE PHASES OF CHANGE
William Bridges – *Managing Transitions*

ending

neutral

beginning

WHY NOT MAKE A 'STOP DOING' LIST?

Most churches are far too busy 'doing everything' that churches are 'supposed to do'. Why not avoid the busyness of a full programme? The motto 'Keep it simple, stupid' is a pretty good one for church life. It is better to do a few things well and not exhaust everyone than to feel you have to do everything.

> **Questions you might ask**
>
> - In order to free people up to be involved in mission, what do we need to stop doing?
> - Why do we do what we do?
> - Why was it begun and is that still valid?
> - What could we stop tomorrow and life would go on?
> - How can we make our church less busy?

Face hard realities.
We are in it for the long haul

The number one factor that prohibits change is complacency. If we cannot create a sense of urgency in people, nothing will happen. If all looks well on the surface and everyone is comfortable, nobody will want to bring about change.

In the UK, the reality is of a rapidly declining church. If what is happening to the church was happening in business, there would be emergency talks and serious and dramatic action being taken. For most of us though, life just goes on as normal, in fact, as if all is well. For all of us in local churches there will be hard realities to face before we will be able to change. There are a number of factors that will make it difficult for you to face the truth.

- If your building, however big or small, is substantially full each week
- If you have a building that you own and it is in good repair
- If your budget is being met
- If your services are good and people are ostensibly happy
- If, even occasionally, new people are joining the church

In other words everything looks fine on the outside. The leadership may be aware that they are not being as effective as they want to be but the people will see very little cause for alarm.

The reality is that we are all part of the wider church and over all it isn't doing well. Most of us are not making real headway. Facing an issue of reality is not an excuse for despair but a prompt to ask questions that will lead to solutions.

In most local churches there are areas that are not being effective. Unless we face reality, there is little hope. There Is no discredit in facing the truth. It is the creative thing to do, not an issue of blame, but of a reality check.

Asking questions leads to ideas and ideas lead to the possibility of change and greater effectiveness.

Leaders face issues head on; the hard realities of what is and what is not working. What is fruitful and what is not? Where have you reached a plateau and where are you moving forward?

Key: Face reality, but do not lose heart. It is not the end of the story. It might be the beginning of something new.

Be absolutely honest about your situation without getting depressed. There is a way out but do not pretend and do not panic.

Comparing yourself with how everyone else is doing is the wrong measure.

Jim Collins, in his book, *Good to Great* describes a conversation he had with Admiral Jim Stockdale, the highest ranking United States military officer in the 'Hanoi Hilton' prisoner of war camp during the Vietnam War. In his eight years of imprisonment, he and other prisoners were appallingly treated. He asked the question of Stockdale, 'Who didn't make it out?'

'Oh, that's easy,' he said, 'the optimists.'

'The optimists? I don't understand, I said, now completely confused.

'The optimists. Oh, they were the ones who said, "We're going to be out by Christmas." And Christmas would come and go. Then they'd say, "We're going to be out by Easter." Then Easter would go. And then Thanksgiving, and then it would be Christmas again. And they died of a broken heart.'

Then he turned to me and said, 'this is a very important lesson. You must never confuse faith that you will prevail in the end – which you can never afford to lose – with the discipline to confront the brutal facts of your current reality, whatever they might be.'

Promises of revival around the corner, however sincere they might be, and however much we could do with it, do little except produce disappointment and 'a broken heart' when they are unfulfilled. Many of us may need to face up to the disappointment that has come from false expectations. Revival may well come but it will come as we seek to do our part and if it doesn't, we go on being obedient anyway.

Even if our personal situation looks good, we have to face the brutal fact that we are collectively losing the game. But we will prevail if we face the truth and are committed for the long haul.

If we do not believe that we might as well give up now!

Eugene Peterson coined the phrase, 'A long obedience in the same direction.' If that direction is the mission of God to make disciples, we must press forward however slow it might seem knowing we shall prevail in the end.

Questions you might ask

- What is the honest reality of our situation?

- What is effective, productive and life giving?

- What is going nowhere?

- What are we doing because we have always done it?

- What are the next steps for us to bring about change?

Mission church requires mission minded leadership

A move to mission-focused church requires a major change in leadership style. We cannot lead in the same way as we did in Christendom days. If there is one area that will prevent the formation of mission shaped church, it is leadership.

Winston Churchill proved to his cost that peacetime and wartime leadership are two very different things. What has served us well in the past almost certainly will not do for today.

Paul's leadership in founding churches was inappropriate for their continuation. His single-handed/small band apostolic style handed over to a multi-gifted team leadership.

For a long time the dominant gift in church leadership has been that of pastor which may have sufficed for a period of our history. We should never lose that gift, as the need for what used to be called 'the cure of souls' is needed more and more in these days of huge social and personal dysfunction. That gift though, if in sole overall leadership, will prevent the mission effectiveness of the church unless it is partnered with other gifts. If that pastor has an evangelistic heart, encourages evangelism, and recognises the need for other ministries then that may be a different matter.

Here are some characteristics of mission-focused church leadership

1. **Visionary**. A missional leader must be able to 'see' beyond today and what is to what could be. He/she should have a sense of future about them or they will be unable to lead people forward.

2. **Outward focused**. Whatever name you want to give this, the future leaders of church must have a heart to look out beyond their immediate situation into the world outside.

3. **Team based**. Hierarchical leadership is still common in the church today. Many churches are still vicar/pastor/clergy dominated but this will not do for the missional church.

   You cannot avoid the reality that the early church even at its most expansive and innovative appears to have been led by groups of people. Of course, there were apostolic characters like Paul, but even he travelled in a team. When he handed over the churches formed under his ministry, he appointed elders to lead them. The term is not important but the concept is. Team does not mean uniformity nor does it deny strong leadership but it recognises the need for multiple giftings. Paul wrote to the Ephesians about God's gift to the church of the five-fold ministries. How that is understood may be open to interpretation but the important thing is that we need the breadth of these ministry expressions in the church, primarily to enable the church to be what it could be.

We need team because we need a variety of gifts in the same way you do if building a house.

To establish a church on good foundations, we must have pastors and teachers. To take us forward we need the prophetic, apostolic and evangelistic gifts.

The key is that the church of the future must be one that faces up to the realities of gifting with honesty and encourages each to function in the gifts God has given them. Those churches that grasp the essential call to mission, need to be sure to have gifts in place that enable that to happen not force people to be what they are not.

4. **Releasing**. There's huge giftedness in the body of Christ waiting to be released; a great untapped potential. The purpose of the ministries Paul refers to, is not to do all the work but is to equip 'God's people for works of service' (Eph. 4:12, NIV). This implies that ministry is not to be left in the hands of the few but for all the saints to be involved. These 'works of service' must be seen not just in terms of serving the church but also ministry to the world outside. That is where the church does its ministry. What a great call on leadership, to be releasers.

The old paradigm was as follows:

The church here is the object of ministry

The new paradigm should be:

The leaders release the *church body* to minister to *the world.*

This requires leaders to see that what the members of the church do and who they are. Monday to Saturday is where the ministry of the church takes place. This is the main interface of church and people. Therefore the role of the leaders is to release and encourage the people to see themselves as missionaries out in the world and to prepare them for that. The preparation or equipping is to enable the Christians to act as disciples of Jesus day by day.

If the church is to be effective, leaders must serve by releasing.

5. **Called to an area not just to the church.** Missional leaders feel a sense of call to a locality not just to a congregation. It means their focus of thought will always be how to best impact that community not on just running church. It means that they will always be judging effectiveness in terms of community involvement and impact as opposed to whether the services are going well.

6. **In for the long haul.** One of the reasons why so many churches fail to grow is the high turnover of leadership. This has even been a deliberate policy in some denominations.

The pattern runs as follows: A church has a new leader. They set a new vision and agenda. After a few years the church moves forward together. They go. A new person comes. The church realigns under this leader and often a different vision. And round it goes. The church cannot pursue one thing consistently and it is always trying to relate to new ways of doing things.

There is a direct relationship between longevity of leadership and the fruitfulness of church.

If you have a new leader from outside, ask the question, 'How long are you staying?' If it is for five years or less, it is likely to cause difficulties. A place needs people for the long haul. That at least should be the intention even if God intervenes and moves people on.

 Note: Appoint from within where possible. This assures continuity of vision and purpose.

7. **A heart for unity.** We can no longer afford the 'luxury' of working alone. In the early church there was only one church in the city or town. God has put ministry gifts in different churches which are to be shared. We have a common calling, a common Head and a common enemy. That should be enough for us to work together. The future lies in leaders who are not possessive over their own domain but see themselves and their church as part of the whole church in the area.

Questions you might ask

- Is my particular gifting suitable for mission church?

- What other gifts do I need in my team to be effective?

- Am I prepared to stay for life if necessary?

Avoid the temptation of constant change

We need to learn from others but when we are desperate to see something happen we may well start to look around for somewhere that is successful. Somewhere in the world, there always seems to be a flavour of the month. The church in the West has become extraordinary faddish, following new ideas that mainly come from overseas often from totally unrelated cultures. By all means we should learn some principles but beware the full package.

Often, the structures put in place in other situations are probably there to harness revival and did not cause it. By adopting their methods you may be buying an empty shell. At the present time, we do not have the growth of Korea, Latin America or Africa and using their structure will not of themselves bring their fruit. But the real danger comes in trying too many new things hoping one will work.

We can learn some things from business. It has been shown that companies that were always introducing new ideas with the hope of breakthrough often failed. But steady, continuous progress in the same direction usually brought a breakthrough.

THE FLYWHEEL

Picture a huge heavy flywheel – a massive disc mounted horizontally on an axle, about 30ft in diameter, 2 feet thick, and weighing about 5,000 pounds. Now imagine that your task is to get the flywheel rotating on the axle as fast and long as possible.

Pushing with great effort, you get the flywheel to inch forward, moving almost imperceptibly at first. You keep pushing and after two or three hours of persistent effort, you get the flywheel to complete one entire turn.

You keep pushing, and the flywheel begins to move a bit faster . . . you keep pushing in a constant direction . . . then at some point – breakthrough! . . . You're pushing no harder than the first rotation, but the flywheel goes faster and faster.

What was the one big push that caused this thing to go so fast? It was all of them added together in an overall accumulation of effort applied in a constant direction.

... There was no single defining action, no grand programme, no one killer innovation, no wrenching revolution. Good to great comes about by a cumulative process ... But step by step, action by action, decision by decision, turn by turn of the flywheel that adds up to sustained results.

So writes Jim Collins, again in *Good to Great*, of his observation of businesses that had breakthrough. In most cases it was hindered by constantly bringing in new ideas.

This is not implying that changes should not be made. But it is persisting 'in the same direction' that produces the results. Nor does it imply purely human effort because the Spirit of God works in and with us as we seek to be obedient to him.

In other words, once you have made the changes that help you major on mission, stick to what you are doing. Beware of loads of new ideas flying in. People get disorientated and eventually discouraged by promises of quick fix success. Stay with it and at some point it will break through.

If you are involved in pioneering evangelism and a new church is being developed, keep going until you experience breakthrough. It will come at some point.

This is the day for the hard graft and the long haul. Much of what this generation does will cause a harvest to be reaped by the next. We may never see the full fruit of what we are working towards but we owe it our children and grandchildren to make the changes that will allow them to see the breakthrough.

Let us start to turn the wheel and continue for as long as it takes.

Questions you might ask

- What pressures have we come under to take on the latest idea?
- What changes have we made in haste and regretted?

Do not try to change what will not change

When John Wesley set out to preach the gospel within the Anglican Church he soon realised the system was not going to change to accommodate to him. Soon he found himself preaching outside that context and saw much fruit of it. (Fortunately, he would find a very different reception today.)

When Paul found himself resisted by the Jews, he turned to the Gentiles.

A huge amount of energy can be used up trying to make changes in a situation that doesn't want to experience change. Many people join a church because they like it the way it is. That is why they came there in the first place. So when someone tries to change things they are often met with stiff opposition. It may be that what those people are doing is fine for them and they are best left to enjoy it. There will be some situations where to continue the change process will only produce misery all round. In other situations it is a matter of time and careful handling.

A way forward that provides much less hassle is to start new alongside the old. Many churches have found that rather than disrupt their present regime of services, they start another that is particularly geared for a specific group of people. Those that want to can then switch to that, and everyone is happy.

Remember Jesus said not to put new wine in old vessels. But he also said that the old wine was best! That should make us creative rather than critical.

A vicar asked us what he should do. His morning service was going well but it was very traditional. Nobody wanted to invite friends and those visitors that did come found it very boring. It was suggested to him that he kept the service going, got someone with vision for it to run it, so that he concentrated on a new second service that would be visitor friendly. Now both go side by side and many new people are joining the church.

We heard recently of another church that had a very elderly congregation, increasingly small in number but nevertheless committed, at their 10.30 morning service. New people were starting to come but any hint of change was objected to by the old-timers. The minister acted very wisely. He approached the whole group and asked for their help to solve his problem. He told them he in no way wanted to change their service but the new families wanted a different type of service. To have a service at 11.30 was too late for children, so what could be done? They realised that they were all up early so suggested they move to 9.00 a.m. and he start something else at 10.30. Everybody was happy as they felt it was their idea.

There are a lot of people tied up with running things in church that they do not want to be running. It is too emotionally costly to try and make the change, so they continue and become tired and discouraged because it Is not what they really want to be doing. You will only really feel the wind in your sails when you are fulfilling you passions and gifting. So never blame other people for you being trapped. Where there is a will there is usually a way. One way is to start a 'fresh expression' inside the existing structure

. . . and it is important not to hurry change where you can make it.

Having said all of the above, in many cases change can be made but we better do it slowly, probably much more slowly than we would be inclined to do. If you are a leader and you have an idea, you want to get on with it. But the majority of people are on the curve somewhere between early adaptors and late adaptors. At either extreme are the 'let's do it now' people and the 'over my dead body' brigade. Most people are not against change, they just need time to buy into an idea. It is well worth getting the majority on your side and often the people to spend time with are the influencers, especially if they think they are part of the driving force behind the change. Involving people in the decision process reaps great rewards.

Questions you might ask

- Where are we banging our head against a brick wall?

- Where is there strong opposition to change?

- What can we start alongside the old so we don't need to be held back?

- How can we graciously treat the group that does not want to change so that we have a win/win situation?

- How have we involved people in the change process?

Look for life on the margins and fan it into flames

In every church there are fidgety people. They give you the feeling they are not really settled. They often ask the difficult questions about why this or that cannot be done. They are easily labelled as 'rebellious' and indeed some of them are and should be encouraged to move elsewhere if they are unhappy. Be careful though that you don't miss the people through whom new life might come.

New things often spring from the margins and a wise leader is humble enough to recognise this. A heavily hierarchical form of leadership will usually not allow room for this kind of initiative. A wise person will be looking for it, listening for it, letting it find expression but building in clear accountability along with empowerment.

This is where much of the new initiative for what the church could become is going to come from. If the present church leadership does not recognise this, these people will either be squashed and go off and do something else or they will set up their own thing devoid of any boundaries. This will result in all sorts of weird and wonderful things, most of which will not last long. In a time when the church has got to reinvent itself to survive, it will be all too easy for the status quo to remain until it is too late. It is common for leaders to feel that if they didn't come up with the idea it cannot be right! It is also common for those on the margins who want to be creative to assume that the leadership will try and stifle it. It is often the younger ones who want to branch out.

The wisdom of age should always be paired with the vision, passion and creativity of youth.

Most new life comes from the edge not the centre. Some of the most creative ideas and venture will not come from the leaders but from creative people on the fringe of things. Embrace them, encourage them, empower them and hold them accountable.

EXAMPLES FROM RIVERSIDE

Riverside Real football team which has had a large impact in the Birmingham football league was not the idea of anyone in leadership but a member of the church with a passion. He shared with the leadership what he wanted to do and was freed to get on with it as well as being given some financial resources. It has had a clear missional impact even if it hasn't won too many games!

The Stay and Play group was the vision of a bunch of mums who were encouraged to go for it. They were resourced by the church and encouraged to have a go. It has proved an excellent way of contacting non-Christian mums and their families.

Both these examples could have failed but in one sense it would not have mattered. At least someone with vision and passion wanted to do something creative to serve the community and reach people. There is no stigma in failing. It is better than not ever trying.

Don't just tolerate new ventures. Encourage them. If they are inside the present structures or a completely new expression of church, give space for people to experiment and take risks. Give empowerment and encourage accountability.

Questions you might ask

- Where are the places of life and the people who are sparking?

- What risks are we taking?

- Where are we held back by 'What some people will say?'

- How have we built in accountability as you have empowered people?

- Have we been willing to let go of control?

✓ Keep it simple, reproducible and low maintenance

Many new initiatives fail because they start off far too ambitiously. To begin with, everyone is enthusiastic so they don't mind putting in the hours and working hard. But, because the expected breakthrough is a long time coming, people begin to lose heart and energy. The project peters out and it becomes difficult to start again.

Alpha type events are a great example of a mission strategy that is simple, reproducible and low maintenance.

On the other hand, events that are reliant on modern technology are brilliant for exciting communication but tend to be very resource-intensive and can rarely be maintained over a long period without a lot of people involved.

Whatever you start you need to be able to complete and you must reckon on the long haul for most mission initiatives.

SIMPLE

The simplest schemes are usually the best. When you look at times when the church has grown fastest, it was usually when life was simple. It is amazing to think that there was no PA to set up, no literature to give out, no PowerPoint or overheads to organise in the early days of the church but they did OK.

Today the Chinese church grows apace in its enforced simplicity.

I am not suggesting for a moment that we should not make best use of modern technology but we need to realise that effective ministry is possible without it.

It is necessary to have to sacrifice excellence because of simplicity.

Wesley did pretty well with a horse and a Bible! Mind you, today he would never have got away with it with all the regulations for holding meetings!

REPRODUCIBLE

If we find something that works well, the likelihood is that it will work in a number of different situations. If it is not too complex, it can be reproduced. To be able to do that saves huge amounts of time, energy and manpower.

LOW MAINTENANCE

Again, some situations require a lot of work in the early stages. A good principle though is to make sure it can be kept going in the long run because it does not require too much in the way of manpower and resources to maintain it.

Questions you might ask

- Can we sustain what we are doing in the long term?

- What are we doing that is easily reproducible elsewhere?

- Have we become too complex to do it well?

Put the right people in the right place

It has been said that people are your greatest asset. That is not true because if you have the wrong people doing the wrong thing, it leads to hours of time given to coaxing, encouraging and pushing. If, however, you have the right people doing the right job, you will not have to motivate them.

You will never achieve your vision by continually pushing the wrong people.

You will never have to motivate gifted people in the right place.

> *Key: Find the right people. Let them loose in the area of their gifting and passion and they will not need pushing.*

Finding motivated, gifted and inspired people and letting them go in the area of their passion is the most important job of leaders. Something will happen because they will motivate themselves. Helping people find their gifts and passions and releasing them without control but with accountability is the most important job of leaders.

If every person, filled with the Holy Spirit, were fulfilling his or her God-given role, then God would be getting done what he wants. The function of anyone at any level of leadership should be to help discover, release and empower the gifts of those for whom they have responsibility.

Churches later in the book have marked this as a key in moving their churches forward. It makes perfect sense. For many leaders, though, finding anyone to help is better than no one as there is so much needed to see jobs filled in the church. But this is a very short-sighted way to behave. It only causes struggle in the long term.

It is always going to be more fruitful if the ministry is shaped around the person than trying and make the person fit the need.

In the light of this,

Questions you might ask

- Are we starting with the people or with the job?
- Who is in the right place and who is not?
- Are our staff doing what suits their gifting?
- Who can we rely on and who do we always have to chase?

The future is in listening to, encouraging and releasing the young

We are in a period of unremitting change. It is a gradual process and the age group being most affected are the young. Increasingly, young people will grow up with only a scant knowledge of Christianity and almost no experience of church. They are the ones who were born into this state of constant change and they handle changes in technology so much better than their parents. They understand their own post-modern world.

What is striking is that wherever you attend a meeting of 'Christian leaders' they will be in the main over forty years in age. Yet, the age group most distant from church are the under forties. It stands to reason that younger people are going to be in the best position to understand and infiltrate this post-Christendom world than those of us who are older.

As well as that, it is the young who are so often full of passion, energy and vision.

It therefore stands to reason that young people should be in leadership in church. Of course they need the wisdom of years working with them but they must be given their heads.

A serious change must take place before it is too late.

THE NEED FOR FATHERS AND MOTHERS

Today we need parents in the faith, parents who will give the wisdom and experience of their years. At the same time as older folk releasing and encouraging the young, the younger leaders would do well to acknowledge their need of older mentors and make the most of those who have experience. But those same people who provide that support will need to acknowledge their serious limitations when it comes to impacting the present younger generation.

RELEASE THE YOUNG

The future of the church depends upon the mobilisation and enthusiasm of young people. Men and women in their twenties and thirties are quite capable of taking leadership roles in churches, church plants, new expressions of church, or new congregations. All they need is some guidance, accountability and wisdom from older people.

They will make mistakes but that is vastly better than not doing anything at all. Let us who are older not forget how many mistakes we made along the way.

A TIME FOR COURAGE

This requires courage from an older group of people to actively look for, encourage, release and resource a younger generation into the work of mission and church leadership. If this does not happen, we are lost. There is very little hope for the church in Western Europe without the energy, drive, vision and courage of younger people.

ADVENTURE WHILE YOU ARE YOUNG

Those of you in your twenties and thirties need to see this period of your lives as a time of huge opportunity for service. If all you want is to get married, settle down and have children, don't kid yourself that at some later date you will be ready to do something particular for God. You may well have died inside a long time before then. There is nothing wrong with marriage and family. It is a great thing, I assure you. In fact, marriage and family can be a way of serving God, but there is much more besides. But do not let it stop you serving God. Set out to do something adventurous with your faith. You do not need to be in 'full-time Christian work' for this. There are plenty of people 'doing exploits' while working in ordinary employment. A friend of ours, in the course of being a teacher and then a head teacher, planted two churches.

Questions you might ask

- What is the average age of our leadership team?
- Which under-thirties have we released into leadership?
- How are we preparing for the next ten years to release young leaders?
- What are we now going to do to give some younger people responsibility?

Children, also a key to the future

It would be impossible to overstate the importance of reaching children for Christ. If we are going to see a generation emerge who live godly lives, it will be because something happens to our children. A number of churches across Europe have grasped the huge potential for impacting the lives of young children and have released people and resources to do it. Of course this, as with anything else, can only be done with people of passion and gifting to do this work. But if it is seen as important, we will start to pray for these people to emerge and be released.

There is a clear historical president for believing this. One of the major fruits of the revival under John Wesley and others, which produced huge social change in its wake through men such as those in the Clapham sect, was the growth of the Sunday school movement. This in its turn became a great influence on the moral state of the nation, being a factor in causing crime reduction on massive scale. A 40 per cent fall was reported from the mid-nineteenth century to the early twentieth century. (Statistics quoted in *Prophecy Today* [Vol 14. No. 2] from an article by Professor Davies, published by the Social Affairs Unit in 1992 entitled 'The loss of virtue: moral confusion and social disorder in Britain and America'.)

The Sunday school movement was dedicated to teaching the importance of reading the Bible, understanding the nature of sin and its consequences and the way of forgiveness and new life. (Often these paved the way for day schools, founded on similar principles, to provide Christian education for the children of ordinary people.)

By 1888, three out of every four children in England and Wales were in frequent attendance. At that time, almost one fifth of the entire population was enrolled.

As attendance at Sunday school increased, so did the living out of biblical perspectives by individuals and their incorporation into society at large. The fact that social ills declined over this period is hardly surprising: the seeds sown so widely were bearing fruit.

Professor David Martin has shown (*Prophecy Today*, Vol. 14 No. 2) that even by 1957, 76 per cent of those over thirty years of age had attended Sunday school at some stage, but of those younger than this only 61 per cent had attended.

This signals another important element of change. In the same way that increases in the impact of the Sunday school movement were followed by social improvement, its decline was followed by social and spiritual decline. And so it has been since that time.

Contrast all of this with what fills the lives and minds of young children today. So many hurt and damaged by divided homes and physical and verbal abuse. Their minds only have TV, children's magazines and videos to feed them, alongside what they receive in school. They are brought up in almost total ignorance of the love of God.

Most churches today, run Sunday school for their kids. It is more likely to be called children's church, or something similar. But in the main, it will be designed to cater for the children of Christian parents and it is right that those children should be taught and cared for.

The main mission programme of the average church will be geared to adults. In only a very few cases does there appear to be an intentional decision, backed by money and personnel to reach children of non-Christian families. There are still quite a large number of non-Christian parents who, although they do not want to go to church themselves, would be happy for their children to go.

If we want to impact our nations with the gospel, it must include the children.

Questions you might ask

- Who has a passion for children and could we focus them on the un-churched?

- What could we do to bring in the children from the community?

- What can be done in the local primary schools?

- Are there local non-Christian parents who would like their children to come to 'Sunday school'?

And most important of all . . .

✓ *Prayer must accompany mission*

In an article for *Christianity and Renewal*, I shared that I had decided to invent a new word, 'Prangelism'. The purpose is to overcome a rather strange divorce that has taken place in the Western Church. We have created something called mission which is the occasional activity of many churches and we have taken intercessory prayer and separated it off into the specialist activity of people called 'intercessors'.

I (Nick) had the privilege recently of interviewing a pastor from a very large church in Brazil and I asked him if there were any obvious factors to which he could attribute the growth of his church. He thought for a minute and said, 'I really do not know. The spiritual climate of the country is very open. The two things that I have observed is that nearly all our people are involved in prayer and nearly all are committed to personally sharing their faith and bringing their friends to Jesus.' In other words, they practise prayer and mission/evangelism together, 'prangelism'!

Over the last 25 years, there has been a coming and going of a number of prayer movements. Many of these have prayed faithfully for the nation but have themselves been dislocated from the local church and from mission itself. Alongside this, we have created the label 'ministry of intercession' which is nowhere mentioned in the New Testament. Intercession as an important part of prayer is clearly taught and exercised by Jesus. To label intercession as if it were a ministry gift in the same way as 'apostle' or 'prophets' is to encourage it to become a specialist activity of the few. This, in turn, can lead to the response, 'If I do not have that ministry then that relieves me of any responsibility to be involved.' It would then be left to this rather elite group of people to hide away and storm heaven on our behalf.

But in the New Testament, prayer and the mission of the church are closely linked, not just through the co-operation between a person praying and the evangelist, but very often those engaged in mission were the praying people.

I (Nick) do not want in any way to understate the value of prayer or the value of those who have given of themselves in this way as I amongst many have been the beneficiary of it, but I do, however, want to make a plea for the twinning of prayer and evangelism.

In Ephesians 6, Paul writes about the spiritual armour. He encourages us to 'stand' with our feet shod with the gospel. Standing in prayer here is related to the gospel of peace being proclaimed. There is no indication in Scripture that we are to wage war in the heavenlies in a complete vacuum from engaging in the visible battle on the ground. Moses would have been wasting his time lifting up his hands for hours on end if Joshua had not been in the valley fighting the battle.

So, how does this relate to us today? It means that it is foolish to get involved with mission without prayer and it is of limited value running prayer ministries that are not directly linked into the process of mission. It calls for evangelists who see prayer at the heart of what they do and who are themselves committed to being men and women of prayer. It also requires that those who feel a call to prayer come out of their ivory tower and get linked into something happening on the ground. It is not that easy to be committed to pray for people but it requires a lot more courage to speak to them of the love of God. We could retreat to our prayer closet and feel the work is done. I often have wondered after all the praying for revival that many of us have been involved in and sometimes feel so discouraged about, that God may be quietly saying to us 'Revival will only come when someone takes the trouble to go and communicate to the people.'

When we pray for revival in a vacuum, we often forget that the revivals under men like Wesley and Moody were obviously undergirded with prayer but they happened because someone was willing to get off their backside (Wesley put his on a horse for hour after hour!) in order to tell people that God loved them. Was it the prayer or the preaching that did it or could it be that neither was sufficient on its own? It is often quoted that there is no revival without prayer, but you would be hard pressed to find many revivals without the gospel being preached. Jesus sent us out to preach the gospel. Part of that process must be prayer as we depend on him but it cannot replace the going.

WHERE IS 'PRANGELISM' BEST EXPERIENCED?

Firstly, it is in the life of the local church. Whatever God is going to do on the earth, it will be through the local church. The church began in mission and grew in mission. It has to recover its central calling and that is mission. As it does so, it must also rediscover a passion to pray.

At a local church mission that I was recently involved in, the minister admitted that they had been a lot further behind in their planning than in previous times. This had caused them to give far more time to prayer as they realised how much they needed God to act. It proved to be an incredibly effective ten days of mission with an extraordinary number of people both attending events and wanting to discover faith for themselves. It did not go unnoticed that the greater prayer had resulted in greater fruitfulness than expected.

It was said of Charles Spurgeon that when he was asked for the secret of the success of his ministry and the reason why so many were impacted by his preaching, he would point them to the group of people praying throughout his services in what he called the 'engine room'.

In the church that Nick is part of, they have followed the pattern of a number of other churches and held a 24/7 prayer vigil. They decided to set aside a room on their premises and there were a whole variety of things around the room to stimulate prayer including facilities for writing prayers and answers to prayer for others to identify with. What was remarkable was not only that several hundred people came at all times of day and night and the extraordinary sense of the presence of God in the room but also the element of intercession was very clearly linked to the longing people had to reach their friends. It engaged at a very real level with very real people. The experience of that week seemed to combine the personal encounter which is life-giving to the individual, and intercession linked to the outreach purposes of the church.

Many cities have also given testimony as to where prayer has reduced crime and drug taking. This provides a great foundation for mission.

Secondly, it must be in the life of the evangelist. This includes preaching evangelists, those who use their gift in day to day speaking to their friends and, of course, the rest of the church who have a desire to witness to their friends in the ordinariness of life.

Jesus gives us a great model for evangelism. Everything he did flowed out of his relationship with his Father. In Luke's gospel alone, there are at least seven recorded times that Jesus withdrew to pray and we can assume there were a great many more than that. One can imagine that these were times both of intimacy and of intercession. The effect of that prayer was that he touched other people's lives with love and power.

The apostle Paul, whose evangelistic ministry had such a powerful effect wherever he went, was a man of prayer. In Acts chapter 16, we read of the start of the church in Philippi. In this account we are told of the first three people converted in that city. Before each one came to Christ, we read that Paul was in a place of prayer. Out of his prayer life flowed his evangelistic effectiveness.

It is clear that prayer was absolutely foundational to all that both Jesus and Paul did. There is no indication that either had links to a prayer ministry some place else that was isolated from what they were doing. They were engaged in prayer themselves and had others around them who prayed. They saw that the work of proclaiming the good news of the kingdom required them to be people of prayer, since prayer at its heart is a demonstration of a relationship with, and complete dependence on, our heavenly Father.

In reading the accounts of the Celtic Christians, it is quite apparent that those noted for their fearless mission work, men like Cuthbert and Ayden were themselves also men of extraordinary prayer.

Many of the most effective large-scale ministries of our generation have demonstrated the powerful combination of prayer and evangelism. Billy Graham covered the cities with prayer triplets. Reinhardt Bonnke has praying teams operating throughout his crusades, as does Carlos Annacondia in Argentina. If it is true on the large scale it will also be true on the small.

I remember some years ago leading a mission to a large university in Britain. We were booked to run a meeting in the union at lunchtime. When we arrived it was teaming with young people all enjoying lunch and not looking like they wanted to listen to preaching! The group got up to play but almost none of the large crowd of several hundred students took any notice. When they asked me to speak I said that I did not see much point. I could think of better ways to be humiliated! They said that they would pray and insisted that I go ahead. (It is always easier to send someone else into battle!) As they prayed I got up to speak and as I had predicted nobody listened. Suddenly a student, who had gained a degree of confidence due to an ample supply of drink, started shouting abuse. Sensing a battle, the whole place went completely quiet. For the next 20 minutes, he asked every question you would want to ask about the gospel and everyone listened in rapt attention. It proved to be a turning point in the mission and many students came to Christ in the following days. Out of an impossible situation, God responded to the prayers of a few people to turn a situation around.

Prayer and mission go together.

Food, glorious food

As we have had the opportunity to observe a wide range of fresh initiatives in all sorts of church situations, we have been impressed by the extraordinary number that include food. There is an incredibly important key here for connecting with people who are not yet Christians.

Everybody has to eat. It is a common factor in humanity. Traditionally (although sadly now not always the case) it is the place where families and communities come together. To invite someone to eat with you is to share in a common human experience. To offer food is to give hospitality and welcome. We find neutral ground around the table.

So it is not surprising that it is the easiest, most natural, unthreatening place to build relationships.

This can be seen in the couple who invite their neighbours around for a meal, Alpha courses that centre around food, church gatherings that include food as a part of their Sunday routine or even the 'On The Move' initiative that has provided huge barbecue festivals in most major cities of the world and many towns across the UK.

If you provide food or even just a drink and snack, you very easily create a bridge. Not many can resist the idea of a free meal and the chance to meet other people.

I (Nick) have been involved in a local church mission where there were over twenty meetings in the week. Nearly everyone one of those, apart from Sunday services, were around a meal. There was very little difficulty inviting people because most people feel comfortable being invited to eat.

The actual meal itself, whether it's a full sit-down affair or something much more casual, provides a very easy place to talk. If you have food in front of you or a cup of coffee in your hand, it somehow takes away the awkwardness of what might otherwise be an embarrassing conversation. If we are able to feed people as well as seek to engage with them about faith, we will find we have provided a natural place in which to come alongside those outside the church.

Our guess is that a very large amount of what turns out to be effective mission in the years ahead will be related to eating together. If you're tempted to bypass the idea of food because it is too much work and go straight to the 'meeting', you might be wise to think again.

If you're looking for creative ways to engage with people, you might start by thinking of food.

Questions you might ask

- What events do we now do that would be enhanced by food?
- How could we use meals to provide a bridge with our community?
- What type of food best suits our culture?
- Where have we avoided serving food because it was too much work?

Three non-negotiable principles of church and how they work

What follows here applies to existing churches and new expressions of church.

Firstly, there are a large number of situations where what is required is not a new church as such but a change to what already exists. The question to ask is what can be changed without completely destroying the essence of church?

Secondly, we are writing this section out of a concern that in the real desire to be fresh, innovative, and radical, we do not throw away the very foundations of church that have sustained it through 2,000 years of turbulent history. There is a point beyond which you cannot go without losing the essence of being the church which is the body and bride of Jesus.

There are spiritual forces that continually seek to destroy the church because it is God's primary way of bringing hope to the world. There is a fine line between being creative and being destructive.

WHAT IS CHURCH?

According to W.E. Vine, the word used in the New Testament, *ekklesia* (*ek*, out of and *klesis*, a calling), has two applications when referring to companies of Christians

> a) To the whole company of the redeemed throughout the present era, the company of which Christ said, 'I will build my Church', Matt. 16:18, and which is further described as 'the Church which is his body', Eph. 1:22, 5:23, and

> b) In the singular number (e.g. Matt.18:17), to a company consisting of professed believers, e.g., Acts 20:28, I Cor. 1:2, Gal 1:13, 1 Thess. 1:1, 2 Thess. 1:1, 1 Tim. 3:5, and in the plural, with reference to churches in a district.

BUT WHAT DOES THAT MEAN TODAY?

There are ingredients of what it means to be church that cannot be changed without denying the very heart of what the experience means.

SCENARIO 1

'I meet for coffee at Starbucks every week for coffee with friends and that is my church.'

'We meet before work in one of the offices for prayer and Bible study. I consider that as my church.'

'Three of my work colleagues and I have an email church. It is sort of virtual church. We keep in touch, send prayer requests and share our lives with each other. That is church for me.'

SCENARIO 2

'We have a very full programme in our church. There are activities for every age group and something on every night of the week. We are all so fully engaged in serving in the church, please do not ask me to do any more and please do not pressurise me into evangelism.'

'We have an exciting new building programme. We have promised a huge sum of money and although we will be in debt for years, it has really given the church something to focus on. We are really trusting God in this and praying for his provision.'

'Our church is great. We have fantastic worship and great teaching. I really look forward to the weekend to meet with God. It helps me get through the week as I work in a very godless environment.'

Are these both church? Does it really matter? We think it does.

When Jesus said he would build his church, what did he mean by church?

Is there a difference between 'churching it' as a means of expressing Christian fellowship, and being 'a church'?

It is well understood that major times of change throw up a period of 'chaos' without which we would never be able to move into the next phase. If we are afraid of 'chaos' it may prevent our discovering what lies ahead and we remain trapped in the old. Therefore what we see now as 'emerging' may only be a phase. *If what so-called 'new expressions' or 'emerging churches' are experiencing is merely a frustration with how we do church it will have limited value. If it is born out of a profound desire to be more effective in mission and wholehearted discipleship then the likelihood is that it will have healthy long-term repercussions.*

Strangely, in any fresh approach to church, we would expect there to be a sense of going back as well as looking forward. For whatever church becomes it will feel more like its original form as it is freed from the negative aspects of its Christendom experience. At the same time it is important not to fall into the trap of idealising the early church as if it were 'perfect' and not see the humanness and weaknesses it contained.

A SENSE OF BELONGING

If the Old Testament is a forerunner to the New, then the patterns set down there would direct us as to God's intentions now. In the Old, the people were divided into nation, then tribe, then clan and finally family. Each was a subdivision of the others but each had clear definition in itself and a form of structure in itself. In the same way, the early church could be seen as universal, town-wide (the church in Corinth) and household (the church that meets in the house of) and maybe there were even smaller divisions that we do not know about. It is quite possible that the latter expressed a huge variety in style and ethos depending on its location and leadership. But, each was clearly defined and a part of the whole. Each was a valid expression of 'church' in itself.

So, even though a mission team, fellowship group at work, or whatever, may be for a time expressing church, they are different from the more permanent expressions we have come to know. Donald McGavran, in his writings on church growth, coined the expressions, *sodality (the local fixed expression of church)* and *modality (the itinerant/mobile expression of church)* (See *Understanding Church Growth*, published by Eerdmans, 1987.). This is a helpful distinction as it enables us to give credence to the missionary groups that function for a limited time but still express something of church. Although in a renewed period of mission in the church's life, we may see more of these missionary bands, most of what we are dealing with here falls into the more permanent category.

SO WHAT REALLY CONSTITUTES CHURCH?

IN THE BEGINNING

When the Holy Spirit came upon the first Christians, there was an immediate, spontaneous and unplanned response; they met together and expressed church. It was an automatic response to God's empowering work that hadn't yet been spoiled by human hands. It gives us a clue as to what Jesus meant when he said that he would build his church.

Much of what happened in this immediate gathering was based on meeting the need raised by effective evangelism.

There were at least three key elements:

- A concern to embrace those looking for God (MISSION)

- A corporate desire to know God and to worship him together (SPIRITUALITY)

- A commitment to live together that went beyond superficial friendship (COMMUNITY)

These seem to be the three principle ingredients around which things like time, place and pattern take a secondary place. They need to be flexible around the central core of a group of people *who love God, love one another and love the world of people.*

Structures, buildings and form are of secondary importance.

If we can discover the heart of being church, it will mean that already existing churches can feel free to discard what is unnecessary and new churches can aim not to come short of all that church was intended to be. In the early church, the 'church that met in the house of' was as valid an expression of church as the thousands who gathered in Jerusalem after Pentecost.

The next part of the book looks at these three key principles.

As you go through it ask yourself

'Do I recognise these principles in my church?'

'What would I do if I could start again?' Even if you cannot begin again, it will help you realise what the important things are and what is secondary.

'In what way can I start again?' Where could you do things in a fresh way and what can you discard?

'Why do we do what we do?' What is the principle behind your activities?

'What should we leave alone? What could we change? What could we start new?'

Mission . . . love for the world

In this part will have a brief look at why mission is an essential part of being church. We also examine some key components of a church's mission.

We will be looking at:

- **Releasing the scattered church**
- **Refocusing the gathered church**
- **Some possible ways forward**

1. Mission

JESUS WAS SENT WITH A MISSION

'As the Father has sent me . . .'
(Jn. 20:21, NIV)

' . . . the Son of Man came to seek and to save what was lost.'
(Lk. 19:10, NIV)

' . . . God so loved the world that he gave . . .'
(Jn. 3:16, NIV)

THE HOLY SPIRIT WAS SENT WITH A MISSION

'The Spirit of the Lord is on me for he has anointed me to preach good news to the poor.'
(Lk. 4:18, NIV)

'You will receive power when the Holy Spirit comes on you; and you will be my witnesses . . . '
(Acts 1:8, NIV)

> THE CHURCH IS TO CONTINUE THAT MISSION
>
> *'As the Father has sent me, I am sending you ... '*
> (Jn. 20:21, NIV)
>
> *' ... go and make disciples of all nations ... '*
> (Mt. 28:19, NIV)
>
> *' The church exists primarily for its non members.'*
> Archbishop William Temple

The early church was *born out of mission*. Peter preached on the day of Pentecost and thousands responded.

It *continued in mission* ' ... the Lord added to their numbers daily those who were being saved.' (Acts 2:47, NIV). It was dispersed because of persecution and immediately engaged in mission '[They] preached everywhere they went' (Acts 8:4, NIV).

The first few centuries saw the church expanding across the known world through missionary endeavour.

Even though it went into the background for long periods of the 'Christendom experience' there have always been groups breaking through, often at great personal cost, to bring the missionary heart of God back into view.

If we are to be the church that God intends us to be and not only survive but be influential at this period at the beginning of the twenty-first century, we in the West need to put mission back at the heart of the church's life and agenda. We can no longer afford just to do mission – we need to be mission.

Mission is that sense of being 'sent' to people outside of ourselves, who need to experience the love of God.

So, if you are part of an existing church, to be authentic means that mission will be at the church's heart.

The same will be true of a new gathering of believers, however small. To be authentically church, means that it has mission at its heart.

What does it mean for an already established church? It means

1. That the understood purpose of the church has a mission flavour

2. That each department of the church's life – from children to the elderly – has a heart for the outsider as well as itself

3. That the events and life of the church are always inclusive

How can leaders facilitate this?

RELEASING THE SCATTERED CHURCH

Here are some guidelines to help existing churches encourage more people to be able to see themselves as missionaries in their own community.

ENCOURAGE AND EMPOWER MONDAY TO SATURDAY WITNESS
As you talk with people, don't just see them as helpers in the church programme but as people with a living testimony in their world, a story of grace. Talk to them about work and leisure and enable them to see that you value what they do when not in a church service. If possible visit people in the workplace to understand their pressures and to meet their friends. Encourage them to have a prayer group that prays for their work and social relationships.

 Speak often in services and out, of the value of what each person does during the week.

PUBLICLY INTERVIEW MEMBERS
What so often happens is that when someone goes overseas on a short-term mission, he/she is interviewed and prayed for before and after, and heralded as 'one of our missionaries'. By definition if you go across the channel you become a missionary! At least that is the message portrayed and received by most people.

Start regularly interviewing ordinary working members of the church, Sunday by Sunday, expressing publicly your belief that these people are the missionaries. In a short space of time the whole church will begin to see that what they do and who they are during the week is not only as important but may even be more important than what they do on a Sunday.

TRAIN PEOPLE IN PERSONAL WITNESS AND SHARING THEIR STORY
Most people have a terror of what they perceive as evangelism. The truth is that everybody has a story to tell and everyone has the capacity to care and love people. Let's release that resource by training and teaching in an exciting and encouraging way and to take away the false expectations that are so crippling.

 Pray regularly for them. Keep teaching it until it is part of the DNA of the church's life.

LET PEOPLE GIVE TESTIMONY PUBLICLY
Give space for people to talk about their encounters in the community. Every time someone shares an exciting story, it will encourage others. I imagine that the early church gatherings were full of stories, often of persecution no doubt, but also of people who had found faith through a Christian's daily witness.

LET NEW CHRISTIANS SHARE THEIR STORY
When people share their stories of coming to faith, it often evokes the unspoken reaction, 'I know someone like that. Maybe they too could find the life that Christ offers.'

BUILD BRIDGES INTO THE COMMUNITY
Look for areas of need in the local community. Find things that the community needs but does not have and see how the church can provide for those needs. There are countless examples, some in this book, of imaginative ways churches have built bridges with the community.

Parenting courses, pre-marriage, young mums, single parents – these are increasingly places of opportunities to meet the community's needs.

If all you do is wait for people to come to you, you may wait forever. By serving, we earn the right to speak.

The Celtic missionary bands that had such a huge impact across Britain and Europe in the sixth and seventh centuries, brought education and health into the communities that they touched. They not only preached Christ but they demonstrated the love of God to people wherever they went. They did not do it in order to evangelise. They did it because in Christ's name they cared.

Our communities need to know that in Christ's name we care.

Have you done a study of your community?

Do you know what the needs are?

Have you got gifted people who could help meet those needs?

ENCOURAGE WORK PLACE INITIATIVES
Encourage and be willing to resource initiatives that people put on in the workplace. Several companies have run Alpha courses, some carol events at Christmas. These type of events take courage but it helps when people know this is something the church and its leaders are fully behind and cheering on.

CREATE NON SUNDAY EVENTS
Moving events away from Sunday enable more people to feel free to come. There is no obvious agenda to join church. It means the Christians are more interested in them than in joining something. Meals are always a good way to bridge the gap. The many good courses around take advantage of this.

RELEASE PEOPLE TO START NEW VENTURES
Encourage and resource new initiatives outside the normal bounds of church. Don't be afraid of things that are outside your control and don't be afraid of failure. At this time, it is better to let people try and fail than for nobody to feel they are allowed to do anything innovative.

Many members of your congregation are deeply involved in affecting the community already. They may need recognition in this. Their jobs impact the lives of other people. For most this has appeared to be something separate from church. This is primarily the fault of leaders.

These people must be encouraged, privately and publicly, to know that what they do is the work of the church.

REFOCUSING THE GATHERED CHURCH

Here are some ways that the gathered church can be more effective.

UNDERSTAND THE CULTURE GAP

For most Christians who are used to church, there is little understanding of just how alien the normal church service is to people who don't normally come. A friend of ours paid his neighbour £10 a week to attend his church and write down everything he felt was strange and difficult for him. He was amazed and grateful for what he found.

Often, the less structured a church is in its services, the more nerve-wracking it is for the visitor.

If we want people to share their faith with others and eventually bring their friends to a service, we need to seriously consider how we can integrate them in what we do.

The songs will be unknown and in some cases unintelligible. The unspoken expectations of behaviour, the readings and as often as not the sermon, may well leave them confused.

But most new people do come expecting and hoping to meet God. They are spiritual beings and want to know God. They love to hear joyous and meaningful worship and most of all they want to feel welcomed by a loving community. They will be encouraged to come again if they perceive that someone, particularly a leader, knows how difficult it is for them, knows they are there and are glad they came.

MAKE PEOPLE FEEL AT HOME

Explanation makes all the difference. When somebody explains what is going on, that it is OK not to understand and normal to feel out of it, this makes a huge difference to the person.

Look at everything in the light of visitors. If we are not willing to do that then we probably don't care if they are there or not.

The people who welcome on the door are key to a person's feeling of well-being.

A drink and refreshments place provided for new people with an opportunity for them to meet some of the team is really helpful if it is done sensitively.

SPEAK NORMAL ENGLISH

Most of us have no idea how much jargon we use in our Christian-speak. Listen to yourself. Ask others to correct you. Avoid in-jokes. Try and be as normal as possible.

 Most church culture is not Christian culture – it is church culture.

EXPLAIN

Readings often need explanation as visitors may not have much Bible knowledge today. If you read publicly from the book of Zechariah without any explanation you might as well be reading from Greek mythology for all they know!

Another might be the 'peace'. Can you imagine a first-timer arriving at church and half way through, just as they feel how well they are doing, the vicar says, 'And now we'll share the peace with one another.' Panic. 'What is that? Is it a piece of paper, a piece of cake or a piece of your mind?' It means nothing without explanation, no matter how clear it is to those who have done it for years.

 Explain the 'obvious'.

BE INCLUSIVE

When you say, 'as you all know', or 'this is a familiar song', or 'as we always do', you exclude all those who have no idea what 'we always do'.

If you ask people to 'see Geoff afterwards' It is only OK if you know who Geoff is. Always assume there are people there who do not understand, and even if there aren't any people like that, at least the message goes out to the church-goers that if they were to invite a friend, that friend would be respected.

FOR MANY THE GAP IS TOO BIG

So many of the people for whom we are praying to become Christians in the years ahead know nothing of what goes on in church. Nothing means nothing! Nothing at all! They've never been there. Think of that. We are helping people into a completely new experience.

 That is why for many people fitting them into existing churches will not work. For many people it is just is too much of a jump for them and for us. We will have to meet them in a new context both for us and for them.

SOME POSSIBLE WAYS FORWARD

There are two possible ways forward.

1. A NEW CONGREGATION WITHIN THE PRESENT STRUCTURE

This might be:

- On a different day
- At a different time
- In a different style
- For a specific age group
- For a different people group
- With different leadership
- In a different place

2. A NEW CONGREGATION OUTSIDE THE PRESENT STRUCTURE

This might be:

- On a housing estate
- In a pub
- In a café
- At work
- Anywhere, anyplace, anytime.

This might be a totally new work.

It might be a development from an existing house group.

It might be a group hiving off from the church into a new area.

It might be a clone of the existing church.

It might be completely different in the way it expresses itself.

It might be any of these things. But the heart of it will be an attempt to meet people where they are and rediscover what being church really means.

All of this involves risk taking and moving out of our comfort zone. The Bible encourages us that miracles follow acts of faith. It is often only by stepping out that you experience God's miraculous provision.

Questions you might ask

- How can we make our gathered church an easier place for new people to feel at home?

- How do we integrate them into the church?

- What new congregation would we need to develop and for which group of people?

- Who can we release leadership to?

- How will we budget for new developments?

Spirituality . . .
love for God

In this part we will look at why spirituality is an essential part of being church. We are using this word to describe our corporate relationship with God.

We will be looking at encountering God in:

- **Worship**
- **God's word**
- **Prayer**
- **Sacrament**

2. Spirituality

We are using the term spirituality to express the part of church life in which we engage with God together, as opposed to relating to one another (community) or to the outsider (mission). We recognise the importance of an individual experience of God and that worship is firstly a lifestyle (Rom. 12:1). But the New Testament goes further and sees the need for us to meet with God in a corporate setting.

The description of the first church in Acts 2 gives us an indication of the elements of encountering God in this way. Paul's instructions in 1 Corinthians 14 where he instructs the early church in some principles of corporate worship, warns against the temptation to individualism.

Some may well think that 'spirituality' is the wrong word! What we are underlining is the importance of encountering God and engaging with him in a corporate way. That is part of the joy and privilege of being the body and bride of Christ. This is corporate worship.

WORSHIP

Worship has become associated with singing songs, which may well be or not be, part of it but it is so much more than that. An act of worship is everything that happens when a group of people come together to corporately engage with God. We know very little about early church worship, which might be just as well or we might be tempted to copy the model. But we know they gathered together in large and small groups to learn, to share, to pray, to break bread and almost certainly to sing.

Justyn Martyr gives us a feel of it from what he wrote in Rome in AD150. He tells us that they had prayer, a reading from a portion of the Scriptures 'as long as time allows,' followed by a discourse given by someone in the church to encourage them to imitate what was heard in the Scriptures. They would then stand, pray, and take communion. Then they would leave for work. It was very simple, uncomplicated, intimate, upbuilding and participatory.

The Greek word for worship, *proskuneo* means to 'kiss towards'. In Hebrew the word, *hishahawah*, means 'a bowing down'. The English word comes from the shortened form of 'worthship', in other words expressing what someone or thing is worth.

Supremely worship is for God.

There are all sorts of forms of worship being expressed today, from the meditational and contemplative to up-tempo and loud. Neither is right or wrong provided that the heart of it is Godward.

We need to keep something of this original purpose in mind when we think of worship in the church today, whatever form the church takes. We can evaluate worship, but not by the usual criteria, 'Did I enjoy it? Was the band good? Was the sermon too long?' but as to whether God was honoured, whether we encountered God and whether we are more equipped to live holy lives.

Corporate encounter includes

GOD'S WORD

ENGAGEMENT WITH SCRIPTURE

The early church devoted themselves to the teaching of the apostles because together they wanted to learn how Jesus would have them live. They had no Bibles as we do but those from a Jewish background only had knowledge of the Old Testament, having relied until then on teachers in the synagogue for its interpretation. Now they had new teachers, ones that had been taught by Jesus himself, to pass on all that he had said.

As things developed, the gift of 'teacher' emerged in the church, probably linked to that of 'pastor'. The gift of teacher assumes the importance of corporate learning.

The call to 'make disciples' also assumes the corporate nature of learning together.

In his first letter to the Corinthians, Paul gives us one of the only glimpses we have of some of the things that went on in an early worship gathering. This was almost certainly referring to a house-size gathering. It may have been in the larger gatherings of the church that preaching was more common but here it was the custom for everybody to bring something in order to encourage others. There is no suggestion that teachers did not also teach. We know that in the Antioch church there were many teachers and this presumably would have been the case elsewhere.

Note: He was also concerned for the 'unbeliever' to feel at home.

PREACHING AND TEACHING

Preaching is the proclamation of truth.

Teaching is essentially the ability to enable other people to learn. The emphasis in teaching is not the teacher but the taught. How people learn will change with the times.

If a 40-minute homily on a Sunday morning was once a good way for people to learn, it may not be today. The issue is whether or not it helps people learn and so to grow.

If challenge through teaching or preaching does not result in change, does it have any real value? What is the point in listening to long sermons if they do not enable growth in a person's life?

The key issue here is how we engage corporately with God's word today so that we can learn and grow together even if we will have to apply it individually. How can the gift of teacher best be used in the modern context so we all benefit?

If learning is the key, then is the sermon the best way to go about it? The answer may well be 'yes' but we'd better be sure. What if after each point in a talk, we all got in groups to discuss it and give feedback?

These are key questions to wrestle with. We must not be afraid to think in fresh ways.

The purpose of this chapter is not to investigate new and different methods of teaching but to challenge us not to feel precious about what we have always done.

We do want to make a plea though; not to be so 'new' in our expression of church that engagement with God's word is seen to be a thing of the past. We need to be very careful that we do not inadvertently buy into the post-modern mindset that anyone's truth is as valid as another and therefore we find our own way without a map.

If the only thing we do when we come together is spend time engaging with God personally, we have not expressed what it means to be church. We have merely fostered a purely private faith albeit in a public setting.

Post-modernity may be helpful in many ways to throw off our rigid forms but if we give in to its demand to please the people we will only serve to lead them further into confusion. Even if we are seen to be narrow-minded, we have to bring people back to the plumb line of truth contained in Scripture. We are strongly urging that we do not lose respect for the authority of Scripture as a guide in our lives and as a primary means by which God speaks to us. What else do we have to say to a lost and bewildered world if we cannot offer them a route map?

Remember the words of Jesus about building on sand and rock. We need to help a storm-tossed generation to build on this rock of simple obedience. And there is no rock except Jesus and obedience to his words.

Preaching will always be needed as a means of expressing the gospel because those outside of faith will need to hear the good news. Many are finding fresh ways to put across old truth in a way that the present visual generation can hear, see and understand.

It will be exciting to see in the years ahead how we learn a whole variety of ways to supplement the preaching of the gospel with innovative ways to learn. We can then be transformed by letting the word of God 'dwell in [us] richly' (Col. 3:16, NIV). After all, if the church is to express the incarnation it will be because all of us seek for the word to become flesh in our own lives.

PRAYER

Prayer is the primary means by which we engage with God. The early church had learnt from Jesus the value of personal, private prayer as a means of developing intimacy with the Father. But alongside that, corporate prayer plays a significant part in the life of the early church. *Prayer in this sense involves intercession, petition and listening to God.* It would appear that prayer was a regular part of the gathered church life as well as on crisis occasions, such as recorded in Acts 4. It is in prayer that we talk directly to our heavenly Father. It is the ability to pray that demonstrates the huge privilege now opened up to us through the cross. It is in prayer that we witness to the reality of the new and restored relationship with the living God. We can now come 'boldly' into his presence.

It is often through prayer that the unbeliever is caused to face the reality of a God who is, who loves and can be known.

SACRAMENT

Sacrament is another means of engaging with God. We know that after Pentecost, breaking bread together in accordance with Jesus' instructions was a common practice. It would appear that this also happened at meals or 'love feasts' as well. Regularly remembering his death and sacrifice through bread and wine, is vital to any expression of church.

Baptism, also, as the initiation into Christ, was an important part of early church life. This becomes more and more important today as people are coming to Christ from a non-church background. An increasing number of those coming to faith will not have experienced infant baptism and so the issue of re-baptism (a cause of concern for some) will become less and less of an issue of contention.

CORPORATE ENCOUNTER MAY ALSO INCLUDE . . .

. . .possibly music. People often express their love for God through the medium of music. It's a God-given means of expressing feeling and emotion in our relationship with him. The Psalms give us a great example of this although we only have the words. Music styles and preferences are as varied as there are humans. Tragically, there is a tendency to assume that the music form that 'I' like is the best for worship. Hence the rather stylised forms found today. Church families are often defined by their singing preference although in any group there will always be a wide variety of tastes so that variety would do well to be experienced in any local church. Many of us like the opportunity to worship in different styles of music.

It is possible though, to worship God corporately without music.

 Note: We live at a time where the 'worship leader' has assumed a high level of importance and many young people aspire to be 'worship leaders'. It is possible for music and even the worship leader to become the object of worship instead of the vehicle. Beware.

Brian McLaren writes from a USA experience

In my travels, I've met a lot of folks from high-intensity worshipping churches who (though they may be afraid to admit it) are getting bored and tired. More is not always better. Louder is not always better. More intense is not always better. The human mind and body need a balance of consistency and order with variety and novelty, and those of us that plan public worship need to attune ourselves to that fact. We also need to get ourselves in sync with the rhythms of our community life which may also be the rhythms of the Holy Spirit. A community may need a latency, a rest period, a time of calm; we're actually out of step with the Spirit if we're trying to keep everyone at least as excited as they were last week – if the Spirit is seeking to lead the community 'to lie down in green pastures, beside still waters' to restore their soul. The converse is true: there is a time and a season for everything – rejoicing, repenting, relaxing, celebrating, grieving, questioning, asserting, and more.

CAN WE MEANINGFULLY INVOLVE NON-CHRISTIANS IN WORSHIP SERVICES?

It is very easy to assume that worship services are for Christians and evangelistic services for the non-Christian. Actually today people are looking for a spiritual encounter not just an intellectual challenge. Provided there is help, explanation and reality, most people will be fine in a worship context. It is important to point out that the majority of non-Christians almost never sing! So the biggest barrier for many will be having to sing, especially if they do not understand the words or do not believe them.

An interesting point here is that it is far easier to sing something you are not sure about when sitting down than standing up. We are almost obsessed with having to stand to sing when it is equally good to sit and sing. It is certainly easier for the outsider because for them it means less commitment at a time when they are not ready for it.

In the eighties and nineties there was a major change in attitude in many churches. They wanted to reach non-Christians by becoming much more sensitive to them in their services. This was born of a genuine desire to introduce people to Christ and to help them grow as disciples. It has been very effective and will go on being so for sometime to come. But it does not suit all.

It is worth noting that it is possible to have something of the visitor friendly that also makes room for encounter with God. It's possible too, to have both of these in the same local church.

> Being sensitive to seekers (his definition of people looking for God) is not a style of worship! I could show you hundreds of different styles being used by seeker-sensitive churches, including surfer seeker-sensitive, artistic seeker services, ethnic seeker services, liturgical seeker services and post-modern seeker services. That's because not all people seeking God are alike. Being sensitive to the mindset of unbelievers is a biblical attitude (I Cor. 14:23) modelled by both Jesus and Paul. It is loving lost people enough to try and relate to them on their level (whatever that is) so Jesus can reach them. (Rick Warren, quoted in *The Emerging Church* by Dan Kimball.)

Community . . . loving one another

In this section we will be considering the importance and the nature of community in the church.

We will be looking at

- **The purpose of community**
- **The small gathering**
- **The large gathering**
- **A helpful pattern: Cell, congregation, celebration**

3. Community

Today, many people who do not want to belong to an institution are longing to be embraced by a community. This becomes more and more apparent in this increasingly fragmented and individualistic world, where local communities are breaking down, families are living apart and loneliness is at epidemic proportions. *And the church is first and foremost a community.*

One of the great miracles of the day of Pentecost was that a group of people from a wide area (most of who would never have met before), came together in large numbers and began to share their lives together in very deep ways. Their devotion and their willingness to sacrifice financially for each other was a mark of that.

God has always wanted family/community. He began with Abraham and his family and then there was an enlarged community made up of families, tribes and a nation, the people of Israel. At Pentecost, a new family was born, the church.

> The church is always community, however small.
>
> It is a community brought together by a common experience of amazing grace.
>
> It is a community bound together by the indwelling presence of Holy Spirit.
>
> It is a community built together through the wide variety of gifts, abilities and personalities.

CHRISTIAN BUT NOT PART OF CHURCH?

Vast numbers of people have left the church, claiming still to be Christians but unable to cope with the institution called church.

As a Christian, you cannot leave the church. You must be part of it if you are part of Christ. 'Leaving' must either mean you have left Christ or else you have chosen to be an estranged member of the church, unable to fully contribute your gifts, missing the joy of corporate worship or fellowship.

There is something very sad about a churchless believer. The problem is that we have so centred church life on attendance on a Sunday that those who struggle with a particular type of service feel they have to leave the church. Everybody loses if that is so.

The church is first and foremost a community of people drawn together by an experience of common grace. In other words it consists of a bunch of people who individually have been wooed by God and been wise enough to respond to his offer of love, acceptance and forgiveness.

THE PURPOSE OF COMMUNITY

WHAT DOES COMMUNITY MEAN?

It surely means a lot more than meetings in which we sing, pray and listen to teaching, however valuable that might be.

It should include

• Sharing of lives

We all need a place of openness where we can be real, honest and vulnerable in the context of acceptance, love and understanding. A place where we will be challenged to live Christ-centred lives and encouraged not to stand still but to move forward in our faith.

• Sharing of food

Eating has always been an expression of relationship for human beings. The word 'companionship' comes from the French, 'with bread'. Companionship is found in eating together. It is a binding factor in all family life.

• Sharing of resources

One of the marks of real relationships of love is when money and resources are shared. That was the mark of the first church and it has been throughout history. Whatever touches your pocket has touched you deeply. When people sacrificially give to one another they have found closeness in relationship.

• Sharing in purpose

The biblical word that we often translate as 'fellowship' is in Greek, *koinonia*. It has to do with participation together in something. When people have a common purpose or work on a common goal, it binds them together. Paul called the Philippian church to a *koinonia* in the gospel. Our common desire to share with others the life that Christ offers, unites us in relationship.

• Sharing of pain

When people suffer together, their lives are bonded together. The early Christians experienced great persecution and suffering, as are tens of thousands of Christians today across the world. In the West we are at present spared much of that but the future could lead us into a greater experience of suffering. But suffering for Christ will bring us together.

What size should community be?

THE SMALL GATHERING

IT MUST BE SMALL

If you are going to have relationships with people at any depth at all, the group you are part of needs to be small enough to know everyone and to feel a sense of family.

It is quite apparent that this was the case in the early church, since they did not in the main, own buildings set aside for 'church', but met in places that were available, predominantly that meant homes.

Paul writes to the church at Rome and says, 'Greet Priscilla and Aquila ... greet also the church that meets at their house.' (Rom. 16:3,5, NIV)

To the church at Corinth, he sends greetings from the same 'church' in Rome.

He writes to the church at Colosse: 'Give my greetings to the brothers at Laodicea, and to Nympha and the church in her house.' (Col. 4:15, NIV)

To Philemon, he writes, 'To Philemon our dear friend and fellow worker, to Apphia our sister, to Archippus our fellow-soldier and to the church that meets in your home.' (Phile. 1,2, NIV)

It is estimated that the size of these churches was about twenty-five to forty people depending on the size of the home. All of these house-size churches would have been part of the church of Rome or Corinth, and would have likely met all together on some occasions.

THE LARGE GATHERING

IT MUST BE LARGE (IF AT ALL POSSIBLE)

I have heard people say, 'I want to be part of a small church.' What they hopefully mean is they want to be part of an expression of church that is small. And so should everyone. But the church on the day of Pentecost was 3,120! And from then on it only got bigger until it was dispersed. God's intention is that the church is large. In heaven we will be gathered in a huge crowd from every nation and tongue. If you only want to be part of a small church, be careful if you join one because you will automatically make it bigger!

We all need to feel the breadth of belonging to the whole family of God, and there are things that can be done in the larger setting that cannot be done in the small. Morale can be lifted, inspiration received, and even the sense of anonymity is appreciated by some. Most new expressions of church are small so they might do well to find other groups to celebrate with. New congregations in existing churches probably would do well to find times when the whole church can do something together and it doesn't have to be a worship service. It could be a picnic or a party!

A HELPFUL PATTERN: CELL, CONGREGATION, CELEBRATION

This has been suggested as a healthy pattern. We only have evidence in the early church of large and 'home' size but there could have been even smaller units. Most growing churches operate at the level of congregation and cell, some emphasising one more than the other as the heart of the church.

CELL/SMALL GROUP

A cell group traditionally consists of eight to 15 people who meet weekly or fortnightly in a home and is led by one of its members. It provides a great means of getting to know a few people really well and of discovering some degree of openness and reality with them. It is a place where sharing, study, prayer and ministry can easily function at a personal level. But even here we easily become rigid. *Why should a cell group be on a weekday evening in a home? It could be any place and any time provided it fulfils the need.*

For some churches the small group/cell has become the focus of church life and the larger congregation less of a focal point. Certainly this would mirror much more closely the experience of the early believers.

It may well be that this pattern may have been forced on the early church due to lack of suitable buildings. The Chinese Church, who have been outlawed from having large gatherings, can only meet in small units, and they have experienced massive growth.

CONGREGATION

Most churches today are congregation size, but divided into small groups to encourage real relationships.

Malcolm Gladwell in his book, *The Tipping Point* (Abacus,2000), reckons that the optimum size for any group to have a chance of knowing everyone is 150. That may be the reason that most churches never grow beyond that number. Once you do, you have moved to celebration. It is no longer a viable size for a meaningful community/congregation.

Many have got over this hurdle in a number of ways.

- Some have started a separate congregation in the same building.

- Some have divided into two or more separate churches.

- In the USA and some parts of Europe, there is a resurgence of 'House Churches'.

  A church grows in a home until it is too big to fit in the house. Then they divide into two, and so on. It certainly has many things to commend it. It seems to work best where those same people get the chance to meet with a larger group from time to time in a larger setting for corporate worship.

- Some large churches have divided the church up into groups that are bigger than the cell/small group but smaller than a large congregation, something closer to the early church house meeting. They have the same feel as the example above except that they retain a celebration event each week or each month. Remaining as one local church, has proved to be very beneficial for the growth of the church and discipleship of the members.

This last example certainly has huge possibilities as far as involving people and in understanding what church should be about. Here is one example.

Example:

One such church gives its reasons as follows:

In this church we have congregation sized gatherings between 25–35 people (enough to fit into a large house) who meet at least once or twice a month on a midweek evening for worship, prayer, learning and sharing food together. They may also meet together for social times. The leaders of these are not necessarily, in fact rarely are, in full-time paid ministry. They would gather a team around them to make sure that the 'congregation' functions well.

Why do we want to run such groups?

We believe this will provide an excellent way for everyone in the church to be fully involved and feel a part of the community to which they belong as well as the wider church. We see it fulfilling at least four roles. Others who have been experiencing these groups for some time have also discovered these.

1. An excellent way into the church

If a newcomer comes to a church service, and sees a large group of people caught up in worship, they may feel intimidated. They don't know anyone and they are perhaps not familiar with the style and/or content of the service. They won't easily feel at home and it is hard to make friends. Making friends is the key to someone wanting to remain in the church.

Equally, if this same person goes along to a small group (of perhaps two to 12 people), looking for a way into the church, they may feel the absolute opposite: painfully visible and highly self-conscious. If, for whatever reason, they don't particularly like this small group, what should they do next? If they don't go back, they risk offending their hosts. And the group members will undoubtedly be at church on Sunday, so they may avoid going to a church service as well!

However, if this same person goes along to a medium-size gathering, such as this, where there are 25–35 people, they will feel neither the centre of attention nor a sense of exclusion. Although the group is small enough to be noticed, it is probably large enough for this person to find someone they can relate to, and large enough for them to be absent the following week without offending anybody. They are free to return some time or they can continue looking around for a community group that would suit them better. Once established in such a group, this person should naturally be drawn into a small group with like-minded people.

2. A great place to make friends

The life of the community group, and the social setting that it provides, should make the forming of new friendships and relationships easier. It will provide a great setting for getting to know new people. Those who are relatively new Christians should find this an excellent way to get to know more people and to grow in their faith. It is the obvious means of forming new small groups and involving those not yet in a group.

3. An ideal setting to develop gifts and ministries

It is very hard to give your first talk to 200 people: it's too overwhelming and too much of a risk. It is equally difficult to give your first talk to five people; it's embarrassingly quiet. Leading

200 strong singers in worship for the first time is very intimidating while worshipping with five enthusiastic but unmusical friends can also be daunting, but for different reasons! It is the same with the gifts of healing, prophecy, tongues, the interpretation of tongues and many other spiritual gifts. The ideal setting in which to develop gifts and ministries is in a group of 25–35 people.

In a congregation people could take it in turns to host the evening, to lead singing, to give talks. And those with the gift of leadership can start to lead.

4. An effective means of church growth

Some have found that the congregation is the ideal group for any new person who wants to join the church. They have the opportunity to meet a group of people and to become involved in the church. Their spiritual life will develop as they start to exercise their gifts, and they will hopefully find friends with whom they start praying at a deeper level in a small group. All these factors should cause their own relationship with God to go on growing.

CELEBRATION

As we have said above, celebration is a gathering of anything above 150 people. It may be, as was the case in Jerusalem, and in many churches today, be several thousand people. It lacks the intimate sense of community that is gained from the smaller group, but is important for a sense of morale and the awareness of belonging to a wider family. It is a huge encouragement to daily feel you are not alone and that the family of God is an ever-increasing body of people. The large gathering enables us to have the great sense of uplift and excitement that comes from a crowd of people gathered for a common cause.

Life can go on very fruitfully without it, as it has in China for so long. We are not dependant on it but it provides a foretaste of heaven and the great crowd that no one could number.

The 7 marks of a pregnant church

A NURTURING PREPARATION

One thing you can be absolutely sure about a woman who is about to have a baby is that she will have the nursery ready. She will be thinking how best to look after the new arrival. Her baby and its welfare will be totally absorbing her thoughts. She will be thinking of clothing, feeding, growth and rest. If there is no place of any sort prepared for the new baby, there is probably no baby expected.

If a church is expecting to see people come to Christ, they will be making changes 'at home' that demonstrate that expectation. If no changes are being made, probably the baby talk is only baby talk.

A SENSE OF EXPECTATION

There is within the expectant home, a sense of excitement and anticipation of the new arrival. No expectation probably means no baby.

An expectant church has a sense of anticipation about it. You can always tell if you have real expectation; you get disappointed when it doesn't happen.

A PROFOUND DISCOMFORT

I am told that to be pregnant and have the baby kicking inside is pretty uncomfortable at times. You can't sit easily with a largely extended abdomen. Having newcomers to church can be pretty uncomfortable and at times inconvenient, but it's all part and parcel of a church that welcomes new people.

A FEELING OF READINESS AMONG INDIVIDUALS

The home (or nursery) isn't the only thing that needs to be ready. The expectant father and mother will have been to classes to prepare for the birth as well as for being parents. A pregnant church will have prepared its members to tell their stories, lead people to Christ, follow them up and be equipped for mission.

A CENTRE OF CONVERSATION . . . ALWAYS TALKING BABY TALK

With pregnant women there is a lot of baby talk around. And why not? It is the most exciting thing in the world. In a mission-based church people are talking babies. They are talking about people coming to faith. They will want to know how we are getting on in sharing our faith, encouraging each other and passing on stories of people coming to know Jesus.

A PREPAREDNESS FOR PAIN AND HARD WORK

Everyone knows giving birth is hugely painful but it is worth it. A mission church is one that is prepared for hard work, disappointments, pain and perseverance because it knows that the joy of giving birth to new Christians is worth it all. Looking after babies is hard work too, and sometimes tests parents to their limits!

AN INTEREST IN OTHERS IN THE SAME SITUATION

It is interesting that when you are in a given situation you tend to home in on people in the same boat. When you are expecting a baby, mums and dads often find others in the same situation to encourage one another. Mission minded churches will find others that they can mutually help and encourage. RUN is one of the organisations that helps to facilitate this.

God wants a pregnant church, ready to birth new believers as he graciously 'gives the increase'.

PART 2

WELCOME TO THE STORIES SECTION!

Stories are immensely powerful. We can quickly forget the content of a sermon, even a good one, but remember the stories for years. Stories put flesh onto words and place us in the heart of the action as we try to imagine what we would do, how we would respond and how we might feel in those circumstances. It was the stories that Jesus told that brought his teaching to life and 'switched the light on' for those who had 'ears to hear'.

Over the following pages you will find a wide selection of stories of how different churches are seeking to engage and impact the culture in which they serve. We have sought to make the selection as diverse as possible whist still keeping the remit of exploring what it means to be a mission church in today's society.

Many of these stories are from new church plants, some are of existing congregations who have begun new initiatives while others tell of those who have just kept faithfully going in the same direction. These are not all 'rocket science', high-flying churches. The purpose of this section is not to present ready made models that can be taken off the shelf but rather to help the process of creative thinking and of developing spiritual imagination. Maybe in reading some of the following stories you will come to the realisation that 'we could do that!' or alternatively 'that would never work for us – but it does give me an idea of what might.'

Most of the churches featured have a website address listed so do visit to discover what the latest news is.

Remember that all new churches and initiatives are fragile – it may be that some won't be around in five to ten years' time while others will have developed into strong, maturing congregations. We are all on a journey and we are deeply grateful to all those who have shared something of theirs with us here.

A number of the following stories are available as video diaries on a DVD produced by a partnership between RUN, Fresh Expressions and the Methodist Church. Those featured have a camera icon on the following page – information on how to obtain the DVD can be found at the end of the book.

STORIES INDEX

WORKING THE NIGHTSHIFT

CHURCH	*HEREFORD BAPTIST CHURCH*
DENOMINATION	*BAPTIST*
CATEGORY	*ESTABLISHED CONGREGATION – NEW INITIATIVE*
LOCATION	*CITY CENTRE*

In the early hours of Sunday morning, Nightshift gets into full swing as night clubbers pour into the Hereford Baptist Church building, the venue to head for after the clubs have closed.

'Nightshift is simple, welcoming, raw, messy, on the edge and risky,' says Antony Wareham, the senior minister, 'yet it is an attempt to be and do church in a different way for those who rarely or never find themselves in a church setting.'

Simple, welcoming, raw, messy, on the edge and risky

Nightshift has developed into a mission project in unexpected ways. It started with the problem of litter, when the answer could have been to put up railings and gates to keep people off the church forecourt but instead two church members in their sixties had the idea of opening up the building, clearing litter and possibly having some conversations with people. This has now led to Nightshift and Hereford Baptist Church building being the on-the-way home venue for two to three hundred night clubbers each week in the early hours of Sunday morning.

Hereford, like many UK cities, has changed over the years, not least with the emerging and growing dance and club culture which transforms the dynamics and atmosphere of the city, particularly on Saturday nights and early Sunday mornings. The mission concept of Nightshift is simple. It is to provide a safe place, a friendly welcome, a free cup of tea or coffee (helpful to some who need to sober up on the way home!), a place to have a chat, maybe to get some help, advice or pastoral support and a way of making church accessible to people who would never set foot inside of one otherwise. By the time people gather on Sunday morning at 10.30 a.m. for worship, church has already been going on in the early hours of that morning in a very different way.

'Hereford Baptist Church,' explains Antony, 'exists to be a vibrant city centre church, which wholeheartedly serves and worships God and where God is at work in people's lives' with a vision to be 'the kind of church God wants and the world needs as we seek first his kingdom'.

The church has therefore recognised the importance of being a living presence for God in the city of Hereford. It seeks to find ways to use its location, building and people resources more effectively so they can relate and communicate Jesus to the people of the city. Part of this has been seeing the church premises open during the week and being a welcoming, attractive place for people of all ages in the community. Four mission action teams have been created, made up of church members with a passion for evangelism, social action, environmental issues or world issues to sustain and aid continued development of mission.

The Nightshift team meets together to pray and have supper before the doors are opened each Saturday evening at 11 p.m., they then work through until 3.30 a.m. on a Sunday morning. Many of the volunteers are close to or in retirement years, and some of the work being done is that of being a 'grandparent' figure to the Nightshifters as they are listened to and have an interest taken in them.

'At Nightshift we often find ourselves having conversations with people who have had some link with a church in the past,' explains Antony, 'it maybe through a youth activity, Sunday school or church attendance or perhaps they have links because they know and recognise one of the Nightshift team.' The team try to respond to a variety of needs, whether it is giving a safe place to hide, somewhere to sleep overnight, help with job applications, finding accommodation or giving some basic essentials such as a sleeping bag and a hot meal.

Christmas and Easter events have been successfully run for Nightshifters using new approaches to sharing the gospel; the church is also experimenting with adapting an Alpha-type course to work in this setting. Other agencies such as the police, NHS and a drugs and alcohol forum are keen to work alongside them. 'We see all of this work as a way we as a church can be a peacemaking community,' says Antony. 'We want to help the wider city and community of Hereford with a binge-drinking culture and the problems that brings to our streets.'

Recently, a number of Nightshifters have turned up on Sundays, especially to the church's Sunday evening café services. One of the most thrilling things for the Nightshift team and for the church has been seeing some of the Nightshifters converted, baptised and becoming part of the church family while others have begun to feel very much a part of the community, receiving support and showing an interest in God.

Coping with the complexity and mess that some people have got themselves into has been pastorally demanding

'How we communicate and proclaim the gospel, how we create the kind of environment for this night club culture to encounter more of God, how we respond to some of the practical needs and issues they face are a real challenge,' admits Antony. 'Coping with the complexity and mess that some people have got themselves into has been pastorally demanding and leading people into a sustained life of discipleship has not been easy with many other distractions around them.'

Through Nightshift, the church has tried to engage with a club culture, not necessarily approving of its values or the behaviour of those who participate within the club scene. There is though a strong desire to connect with people and serve the community around them, flowing out of a distinctive kingdom of God lifestyle and value base. God has used Nightshift to change people's lives and also to change the life of the church, giving it greater confidence, vision and opportunity in its mission to the people who live around them.

Jess has just turned eighteen and is a professional singer:

I always knew that there was something there, but I didn't know how to reach out, open myself up and find God. I was so desperate and hungry to know God like he knows me. But I went through some difficult times and turned to drink.

One night after clubbing out in Hereford, I came along to Nightshift and spoke to people who helped me significantly. I agreed to come along to the service the following night. It was a service all about nightclub culture and reaching out to people. When I stepped through the doors, I immediately felt welcome and content. Now I can't stop coming along to church and I'm completely on fire. My faith grows stronger everyday. I feel that God is calling me to sing and preach the word of the Bible through song and to work with people who are less fortunate than myself. At first I found it really nerve-wracking but I knew it was right for me. I want to feel pure and I want to follow with all of my heart the path and the journey that God has planned for me. Now I know that I can live the life of freedom that Jesus died for me to have. Isn't God amazing?

Les says:

In May 2004, I had a few problems in my life and didn't know how to cope with them. One Saturday night/Sunday morning I ended up at Nightshift and that's when it started. It was a free cup of coffee and a toilet stop to start with. The people at Nightshift made me feel needed and that started me thinking about my life and where I was going, or more importantly where I was going to end up. I continued to attend Nightshift on and off over the next nine months and was invited to attend the café services held on a Sunday evening. I went along; there was a great sense of peace and I felt very relaxed. I was told there was to be a baptism the next week and was curious to see what happened.

I attended the baptism and as I was watching something happened; God spoke to me and told me I needed to have my life turned around and to go his way. I went forward for prayer and accepted God into my life. I felt so happy and content.

My life has completely changed now, and if it was not for the people at Nightshift and having God in my life I don't know where I would be today.

 For more information visit: www.herefordbaptistchurch.org.uk

I DO LIKE MONDAYS

CHURCH	*ST MARY'S, TODMORDEN*
DENOMINATION	*CHURCH OF ENGLAND*
CATEGORY	*ESTABLISHED CHURCH – NEW INITIATIVE*
LOCATION	*TOWN CENTRE*

Church on a Monday in a Yorkshire town with a Lancashire postcode sounds like the basis on which some medieval battle might be fought. Indeed Canon Peter Calvert, vicar of St Mary's, Todmorden, says that church life in this Pennine town at the edge of the Wakefield diocese has never been easy. Maintenance rather than mission has been the rule.

In the early 1980s, Todmorden had to grasp a painful nettle. There were two churches in the parish, a legacy of the nineteenth century, used on alternate Sundays, with many different service times and little sense of outreach to the local community.

A long and difficult five-year process led to the decision to reorder the daughter church and close the parish church. This took another five years to happen, with much prayer and effort, especially in raising the best part of half a million pounds. St Mary's was dedicated as the new parish church in September 1992.

A key factor was the willingness to suffer. Two congregations which had seen themselves as separate entities came together – some were to lose their beloved building altogether, some were to see their building ripped apart. A common sense of suffering was the only way to bring all to work together for the future.

the very stones seemed to be saying, do something, try new things

'I believe that the spiritual and financial suffering brought a new sense of waiting on God,' says Peter. 'The reordered building brought its own challenges, the very stones seemed to be saying, do something, try new things. We wanted to use the building during the week, and a new pattern soon began to establish itself.'

Peter asked people what they wanted and the young mums at that time said they would like something after school. This was how the Monday service started. Refreshments are served, with help from some of the young teenagers, from 3.30 p.m., then the service starts just after 4 o'clock, lasting half an hour. Since 1982 the average attendance has been between seventy and eighty – young and old, babies, toddlers, primary children, and a small number of secondary children. Some children are brought from the church school; others come with parents or grandparents. This service has brought in many people who would not otherwise come to anything.

'It is a simple Eucharist,' explains Peter, 'with a very informal and interactive ministry of the word. Children are at ease with word and sacrament, and adults who would be overawed by the most welcoming parish communion can feel at home on Monday. "We can understand what you're on about on Monday".'

An increased awareness of the changing world around them has made St Mary's think about their pattern of worship. They recognise that Sundays have changed out of all recognition in the last few years, with Sunday work, young people's sports and more broken families. They feel that a range of services across the week gives everybody the chance to worship regularly and although Sunday remains the focal point, the weekday services are a vital part of their pattern. The total weekday attendance is often comparable with the Sunday figure.

'On different days we have communion services at 6.55 a.m., 10 a.m., 12.15 p.m., 4.05 p.m. and 7.15 p.m.,' says Peter. 'The slightly odd times are because we try to fit in with people's needs – so there is a reason for them all. We believe that a key question for us all in our strategic planning is "How often do we actually ask people what their needs are?"'

The buildings are well used during the week, apart from worship. A dedicated band of 'church-sitters', mostly retired people, staff the premises. Peace prayers are said every day at noon, by lay people. The crypt hosts clubs for the elderly, and for several groups of handicapped adults, as well as all the usual church meetings.

'Nothing which happens at St Mary's is particularly startling,' reflects Peter. 'We are a reasonably orthodox middle-of-the-road Anglican parish, striving to relate to the community around us. One of my greatest joys is when visitors or newcomers say that they are attracted by the warmth and friendliness not just of the people, but by the very building. I believe that a building does have a "feel", which is generated by those who use it regularly.'

St Mary's believes that their prime duty as Christians is to worship God and that everything else springs from this. Peter maintains that worship, fellowship and mission cannot actually be separated from each other; they are interlocking parts of our Christian lives and in no sense optional extras.

> The church cannot stand still . . . if we stand still, we lose ground

'Whatever happens next, I am sure that there will be movement,' explains Peter. 'The church cannot stand still. Christian outreach is like walking up the down escalator. If we stand still, we lose ground. If we make strenuous efforts, we can surprise ourselves with just how far we can go.'

Judith's Story:

Living busy lives as we do these days, the provision of weekday services is imperative.

My husband is not a Christian, and therefore sometimes there has to be give and take. For me, to be able to worship during the week is a life-saver. Weekends can be taken up with so many family activities – visiting friends and relatives, climbing mountains (or hills!), or working.

On Monday afternoons I join in our simple Family Communion. The atmosphere is electric, but at the same time it can be very still and quiet – in fact, the children can be quieter than the adults! Children seem to ask the simplest questions, but they are ones to which I have always wanted to know the answer. As a Mothers' Union member I believe in family life values, and know that families need as much support as possible.

On Wednesday evenings we have a spoken Communion. This service is for me the most meaningful of the week. We have a quiet time at the beginning and there is an address after the Gospel. There is much to think about – and time to do it. I help to prepare the altar before the service and administer the chalice. It wouldn't be Wednesday without my communion.

CHELSEA'S YOUNG SUPPORTERS

CHURCH	*CHELSEA COMMUNITY CHURCH, LONDON*
DENOMINATION	*BAPTIST/URC*
CATEGORY	*COMMUNITY ENGAGEMENT*
LOCATION	*INNER CITY*

In the heart of Chelsea is a church that sees about eight hundred people from the surrounding area Monday to Friday.

With a mission to the people of three local social housing developments and dominated by the Worlds End Estate, Chelsea Community Church is a Baptist/URC local ecumenical partnership which has a particular ministry to children and local homeless people.

Working in close partnership with a charity called 'The Regeneration Trust', they run a Community Computer Training Centre. The church is also part of West London Churches Homeless Concern which runs a winter night shelter in church halls from November to April and has recently started a street outreach programme while the night shelter is closed.

Coming from a wide variety of backgrounds, including many from local Muslim communities, the fact that very few of these contacts have any real control over their housing situation means there is a high turnover rate and this in turn is a significant issue for the church.

Graham Watkins, minister of the church, says 'I was appointed as minister when the partnership was formed nine years ago and it felt like the church was restarting. During that time the Sunday morning congregation has grown from about fifteen adults and a few children to a pool of around ninety people who come regularly but not necessarily every week, nearly half of whom would be under sixteen years.' It is, however, through the midweek activities that the church has possibly made the greatest impact.

'The starting point has always been that we would try to bless local children and their families in an area which has a very high proportion of single parents,' says Graham. 'We now have a set of activities for children, young people, local schools, parents and homeless people.

God seemed to be saying to the church that the parents would come through the children

God seemed to be saying to the church that the parents would come through the children and while it took some time to see the fruit of this promise, in the last few years this is exactly what has happened.'

BUILDING RELATIONSHIPS

Chelsea Community Church believes that what they are doing in the local junior schools is highly significant. It also offers a wide range of services through the computer centre, after-school clubs, reading support and weekly school assemblies as well as offering help with one-off events. Ashburnham Community School on the Worlds End Estate has gone from a struggling school to having 'beacon status' in the time they have been working there. Given that 60 per cent of the children come from a Muslim background it is particularly encouraging that the local Islamic communities have supported them holding Christian assemblies and attend many of their activities. The church provides a homework club, 'IT Teens' which is an after-school computer club for secondary school children and they also run Boys Brigade, Girls Club and 'JAM' children's church. Every child who comes to JAM gets a home visit each week which is key in developing a relationship with the whole family. Other groups include Jigsaw Club for parents, Footprints community lunch, adult computer courses, Alpha and a Bible exploration group.

'The result of this level of engagement,' says Graham, 'is that we get to minister to people in the context of their family and community which creates a sense of belonging in an area where the church was closed to people for many years. We believe this is the only context in which we can meaningfully share our faith in this place.'

Samantha's Story:

Samantha is a nine-year-old who heard about Girls Club. Her mother is not well so her grandmother brought her along and stayed for the session, including the short Bible time. At the club they heard about 'JAM on Saturday' (JAM is kid's church and stands for 'Jesus and Me'). Not long afterwards Sam and her grandmother came to church and have basically come ever since. Sam's mother heard about this and also started attending. Both her mum and grandma signed up to Alpha and brought along some friends and relatives to a few of the sessions. Sam's mum organised a dedication service for Sam and invited her friend Mary along to the church. Mary had recently lost her job and so started to come to Jigsaw parents club and did a computer course; she had her son dedicated a few months later. The relationship between Sam's mum and dad had ended some time ago, but when it was discovered that he had become homeless the church was able to help and encourage him into a local homeless hostel. Sam's grandfather has struggled for years with alcohol and depression but recently started coming to church. Sam's mum was baptised a couple of months ago. All of the people mentioned here were previously completely unchurched.

(The names of those in this story have been changed.)

The church has worked hard at being comfortable and friendly with those who are not used to attending it. They accommodate babies crying during prayers and sermons, toddlers wandering about, people arriving ridiculously late then staying an hour afterwards and also seek to meet the needs of homeless or recently homeless people.

'Most of this has been a real positive,' says Graham. 'The most difficult thing is the concept that we have had to ban people from church for a period of time because of their behaviour. We were forced to impose this on a particular group of teenage girls at one point, and twice on people who were ex-homeless. I once had to ask somebody to lead an extended time of prayer while I quietly removed one particular individual!'

VISION FOR THE FUTURE

One major frustration for the church lies in seeing people who have come a long way sometimes slip back, especially *. . . persistence and the building of relationships are key* when working with the homeless, but Graham is quick to point out that these experiences are offset by those whose lives have been turned around and now serve the local community.

The most significant impact of this church seems to have been made through a consistent long-term commitment; it is no surprise therefore that in one sense the future plan is to do more of the same with two specific projects on the horizon. Firstly, a mentoring scheme for boys who have no positive male role-model at home. Secondly, there is a vision for a new computer centre which will focus more on the 'funky youth' end of technology and will include a recording studio and dance floor. The vision is to reach some of the older 'excluded' teenagers who are in danger of getting entangled with the drugs scene.

What has the church learned? That persistence and the building of relationships are key. Graham felt that he could quite easily have walked away after three years thinking that they had done some 'nice things', but realises now that so much more has been accomplished through the long-term commitment. 'I am amazed at the wonderful things that are said about the church even by people who have not joined us yet,' says Graham. 'It takes time to get to know a community and the individuals who are a part of it, but it is worth it in the long run.'

David and Paul's Story:

David, an ex-homeless man, borrowed a table and cloth from the church and cooked lobster and champagne on the Kings Road because Paul, a homeless man, would not come into his flat. David then asked Janet (who organises our children's work) to get the children to write Christmas cards to Paul; David delivered one per day up to Christmas day about two weeks before Paul died. David recently died quietly in his flat.

SUFFOLK PUNCH

CHURCH	*MENDLESHAM CHRISTIAN FELLOWSHIP*
DENOMINATION	*INDEPENDENT*
CATEGORY	*CHURCH PLANT*
LOCATION	*VILLAGE/RURAL*

Mendlesham, an idyllic little Suffolk village has around five hundred and fifty homes and is at the heart of the local farming community. Thirteen years ago 30 people came from that local neighbourhood to the first service of MCF (Mendlesham Christian Fellowship), today the church runs two identical services for the 300 people who attend each Sunday in the village community centre.

The initial vision to start the church came from Steve and Sara Fenning who were working part-time with a local Brethren chapel. They felt that in order for the work to grow, the old chapel should be closed and a fresh start made in the village community centre in nearby Mendlesham. A leadership team of six men and women was appointed to establish this new work. Church life was kept simple, outward focused and family orientated. As the church grew, new programmes developed, staff were added and an office base moved from someone's garage to an old converted chapel.

Early attempts at articulating vision produced a mission statement that was so long and complicated that no one could remember what it was! Two simple and evocative *We want to experience the joy of working with God* words have now been adopted as encapsulating the purpose of the church and have become part of the everyday language at MCF - 'transforming lives'. 'We want to experience the joy of working with God to see hundreds of transformed lives through our church,' says Steve.

Having a clear direction to travel in was important but having the right people in the right places to lead and serve was also essential. They found the rearranging of people into the right places was a vital but painful experience. 'It's never easy having those kinds of conversations, nor was it easy to let go of being a small, family based church,' remembers Steve, 'but in order for the church to continue to grow, we needed to adapt our structures and reshape our serving teams.'

Various staff have been appointed over the years to help move the church forward in specific areas, such as children's and youth work, administration and leadership.

Key values for the church are:

- Learning
- Communicating
- Community
- Involvement
- Growing
- Giving

FIVE S'S

'With a great team of staff and volunteers in place, a clear and memorable statement of vision to shoot for and a set of values clearly identified, our next task was to work out how we were going to get there,' says Steve. 'We came up with our "5 S's" strategy. These became our focus for how we would see lives transformed and gave us a picture of what a transformed life could look like.

'This is how to grow, how to attract new people and connect them into the life of the church.'

SUNDAYS

MCF admit this is what they do best and whether they like it or not, this is often where people form their first impressions of the church and come to see what it's like.

They believe that if they don't connect with people on a Sunday they will vote with their feet and that will affect all the other departments as well.

Steve makes the point: 'If you think about it, every Sunday morning we are in competition with sports clubs, coffee shops, cinemas, Sky TV, shopping centres and a long lie-in! What we deliver every Sunday must be creative and in a language and style that this generation understands. In the past our approach wasn't consistent and it prompted us to change in order to make Sundays a significant hour in anyone's week.'

In recent years MCF has come to realise that increasing numbers of children and young people want to worship and learn with their peers and in their own programmes. So *MCF 242* – a congregation specially designed for teenagers – was started; they are just about to do the same for their children.

SPECIAL EVENTS

The aim here is to provide regular, credible, high quality events, courses and programmes that support people in their daily witness.

There is a volunteer 'Special Events leader' who takes responsibility for leading the various departments such as Alpha, social events and Café Church – a new initiative run on a Sunday morning where the service is video-relayed through to a café setting. Here people can drink coffee and observe what's taking place without having to participate.

'This is proving ideal for non-Christian friends who would find being in a church service intimidating,' says Steve.

SMALL GROUPS

Everybody regularly attending church is encouraged into a small group of not more than 12 in order to develop authentic and accountable relationships. A volunteer leader with a passion for small groups has been appointed to develop a programme of regular teaching, training and support for the leaders and assistants. Currently 88 per cent of those who regularly attend Sundays are part of a small group. MCF believe this is where life change goes deepest and where people learn the value of 'doing life' with others.

SERVING

By providing places where people can have a sense of belonging and ownership, the congregation feels it can play a significant role in the ongoing life of the church. MCF has worked hard to attract volunteers, connect them to the right jobs, train them well and sustain them for the long haul. 'Taste and See' has been a key programme in helping the church to achieve this. It gives people the chance to try a variety of serving opportunities without signing up for life.

SOCIAL INTERACTION

The aim here is to work in partnership with organisations and churches both locally and worldwide to transform the lives of those in need.

This is the least developed of the '5 S's' strategy as a key leader for this area is yet to be appointed.

Everything rises and falls on leadership

So what would be one of the strategic lessons that the church has learned during its journey?

Steve is clear. 'We have learnt that everything rises and falls on leadership. We have an increasingly growing budget for developing and training our leaders at all levels because it's the key ingredient that gets you to the next step.'

A collection of emails that tell the story of how God is transforming their lives through MCF:

Katie, nineteen-year-old:

BLOOMIN' MARVELLOUS!

That's what I think about what you've done at church . . . bloomin' marvellous. The mixture of approaches and styles has worked really well. Each service has made such a clear point without seeming all doom and gloom, instead they have given a sense of hope and encouragement. I've loved being part of it, I've had so much fun, but I guess that's serving at MCF for you!

Grace – retired lady:

You have the gift of keeping the message 'real' which I find so much easier to relate to my every day life.

Andy and Jenny – young married couple:

Just wanted to let you both know that our friends who were visiting us from Nottingham really loved Sunday's service (as did we!). They have taken quite a few ideas away with them to use when starting up their new home group. They commented that 'we've a fantastic church on our doorstep'. We just wanted to say thank you. It's great when friends come and stay, as MCF is so reliable but fresh – hope that makes sense!!

Andy – a prodigal:

Thanks for another moving and thought-provoking Sunday. I never leave MCF or Alpha without feeling I've missed out on so much in life as I've only recently returned to a Christian way of life, and am desperate to grab as much knowledge and friendship as I can to live a healthier Christian life.

Tim – a twentysomething:

I am grateful for the friends that I have gained since coming to MCF and for the fantastic worship times on a Sunday. For the teaching and the spiritual growing talks. For the passion shown by the leaders in God and the way it spreads throughout the church. I am grateful for everybody involved with the church. Thank you God for transforming my life. Thank you for getting me involved with MCF, it has made me realise that church can be so much more than turning up on a Sunday and listening to someone preach and lecture you. I've met some great people and although the church is so big I now feel I belong here. Small group at MCF has helped me grow and explore my faith and helped me to get to know people at a deeper level and make some great friendships. The services are amazing, they are so relevant and informative. Now church and small group are the things I look forward to each week.

 For more information visit: www.mcfsuffolk.org

EASTERN PROMISE

CHURCH	*SANCTUARY, BIRMINGHAM*
DENOMINATION	*INDEPENDENT*
CATEGORY	*NEW CHURCH PLANT*
LOCATION	*URBAN*

'Create a place of sanctuary. Somewhere that I can draw people to, where I can speak to them, where I can draw near and give them space to grow.'

These are the opening words of a prophetic message given in February 1999 and the basis on which Sanctuary was established. From a small group of people praying and arranging events amongst British Asians in Birmingham, came the desire to see something fresh emerge where Sikhs, Muslims and Hindus as well as westerners attracted towards eastern culture could explore Christianity in a non-threatening environment.

Pall Singh, Director of East + West Trust explains how the rest of 1999 was spent in discussion, prayer and planning so that Sanctuary could be launched on the first week of 2000. A team was formed who proceeded to draw out the values and ethos of Sanctuary from the prophecy:

> Come to people with a spirit like mine of acceptance, of love, recognise their seeking . . . be gentle, accepting. Do everything out of a motive of love, as I do.

The focus of Sanctuary is unconditional love, acceptance and forgiveness towards those of other or no faith

The focus of Sanctuary is unconditional love, acceptance and forgiveness towards those of other or no faith. In order to help people feel safe and secure, lighting is low and there is space for private meditation and prayer.

Sanctuary meets in a suburb of Birmingham, outside the main Asian areas in order to be safe for people to come without being seen by their community. The team works hard to create the atmosphere, yet keeps the 'service' simple and uncluttered with plenty of space to connect with God.

Pall reflects that one guest recently commented, 'On entering the hall I was immediately captivated by the peaceful atmosphere of the room with its beautiful eastern décor, haunting Indian music, and the diversity of the people there, many in ethnic costume. The walls and ceiling were draped with sari material, complemented by a candle lit glow that enabled my imagination to meditate on the idea that Yeshu the Light was in our darkness. I had a strong sense that there was a real effort made by the Sanctuary team to address the needs of the British Asians.'

Symbols are very important and powerful at Sanctuary. At one event the eating of Asian sweets during prayer was a significant way of explaining how Jesus brings joy into times of sorrow and pain.

During the last five years a unique, a safe place has emerged as a grace and faith community for east and west to discover Christ without losing their cultural identity. It has provided the means to allow people space to belong before they believe and realise that Christianity is more than just a 'white man's faith'. Those who have discovered Yeshu for all cultures through Sanctuary, enrich the gathering by their presence in prayer, worship, music, fashion, colour and food from heaven!

'Some Christians have a fear of other faiths which is due to the lack of understanding and awareness of Asians,' says Pall. 'It's important to recognise that there is truth and there is error and a limited revelation of God in other faiths. Sanctuary is about sharing Christ, not merely another religion full of rules and regulations. It is based *. . . often people from an Asian background are already on a journey toward God* on the realisation that often people from an Asian background are already on a journey toward God, and spiritually further down the road than their western contemporaries.'

Sanctuary has also attracted those disillusioned and embittered by their experience of church and seeks to point the 'prodigals' back towards a loving Father God.

The church may be small in numbers but depth of character and experience of God have shown themselves and baptism is a huge commitment for those from another faith background. The main

Creating a safe place for people from all backgrounds is a massive challenge

achievement is that the numbers are not merely made up of church transfers but of those who have had no involvement with churches or Christians before.

'Creating a safe place for people from all backgrounds is a massive challenge,' says Pall. 'Acceptance of people despite their lifestyle can be misinterpreted as condoning behaviour; yet this is still the aspect of God's gracious character which is emphasised at Sanctuary.'

Sukhjeet's Story:

Sanctuary has such a special place in my heart, whatever other trials are going on in my life with family, friends or work, Sanctuary for me is the place where I find peace and connect with God. I have been coming along to sanctuary since 2001. I was baptised in September 2002.

I originally come from a Sikh background and it felt safer to walk into Sanctuary than a traditional church setting. I have always been a spiritual person, but always searching for something! When I first came to Sanctuary I was not a believer and in fact was not 'on speaking terms with God'! My family had become involved with worship that seemed legalistic and spiritually unsafe and it took a long time to feel comfortable at Sanctuary. I spent most of my first months there in tears! Despite this I felt a real calling to be at Sanctuary on Sundays. In this place I learned that I didn't need to go through a priest to connect with God or make sacrificial offerings or that God would punish me greatly if I forgot to pray that morning. I learnt that God was for me! I learnt that when I pray, he listens, and that he wants to protect me and see me safe. This is the beauty of Sanctuary; you are welcome and accepted whoever you are and wherever you are on the journey. You are not pressurised to participate in all of the worship.

 For more information visit: www.eastandwest.co.uk

TURNING THE CHURCH AROUND

CHURCH	*MIND THE GAP, GATESHEAD*
DENOMINATION	*METHODIST*
CATEGORY	*NEW INITIATIVE*
LOCATION	*URBAN*

'What are we to do?' was a cry from the heart of the 17 churches in the Gateshead and Jarrow Methodist circuit as they began to realise the extent of decline over recent years and contemplate their future if this trend should continue.

When faced with the reality of rapid decline, many folk may have been tempted to despair, but instead of saying 'it's too late, we can't do anything' the response was 'we must do something... and we must do something now!'

God gave a vision for a new work to Elaine and Stephen Lindridge, two of the ministers in the circuit. They believed that God was asking them to set up a project to work with existing Christians in the eighteen to forties age group in such a way that would attract the missing generations back to God.

We must do something . . . and we must do something now!

It was recognised that it was essential to get alongside those who already had faith but were becoming increasingly dissatisfied with church and traditional worship. This was where the work would begin.

Mind the Gap began in September 2001 with four main elements to its ministry:

- Theophany: a contemporary worship programme.

- Cell: an essential element to encourage people in their Christian lives. Over the years this has resulted in individuals being released into God's work through starting to recognise and grow their gifts in a safe environment.

- Alpha: a tried and tested introduction to the Christian faith.

- Curious?: A seeker-targeted event for those who are 'just looking'.

Each of the areas has a team and the leaders meet together regularly to pray and discern God's will. Recognising that vision grows and changes, they see it as a priority to keep seeking God for continued revelation.

All these different elements link into each other. Cell members are encouraged to meet monthly to worship at 'Theophany' but also to pray for their not-yet-Christian friends and family. 'In practice,' says Elaine, 'many have still found it too big a jump to invite friends to Cell socials or Alpha courses, so instead they invite them to the seeker events – 'Curious?', which are cringe-free, informal social occasions. Alpha remains an excellent course to invite people to should they start to show an interest in exploring Christianity.'

Evangelism works best when it is relational, honest and natural

Mind the Gap teach that it is important to be salt and light in everyday life. 'Evangelism works best when it is relational, honest and natural,' says Elaine. 'Mind the Gap simply set up events and structures that are much more accessible to those with or without faith.'

Central to Mind the Gap are the key values:

- Jesus at the centre
- Every member in ministry
- Every member growing
- A community of love and honest
- Every cell multiplies

Mind the Gap is still fairly small; there is however, an excitement among those involved. 'What is particularly encouraging' says Elaine, 'is that the people now seem to have a higher expectation of what is possible and see that their relationship with God is growing.'

Over the last four years, some have come to faith and been discipled in the cell groups, a handful of who have come from an unchurched background. Mind the Gap has also attracted people who were becoming discouraged in their local churches as they were in the minority age group. Most have remained a part of the local church but are now more excited about their faith. Recently, older teenagers who were in danger of leaving church have been attracted and have found something more relevant to their life and culture.

There are now around fifty people in cell with an average age of about thirty-four.

'We recently made the bold decision to stop calling ourselves a project and take up the term "A Fresh Expression of Church",' says Elaine. 'We fully recognise that one of the mistakes we made in the early days was the presumption that when new people came to faith we would be able to feed them back into the local church. In practice, this has not been the case. Most of the new Christians are totally committed to the work of Mind the Gap, but cannot make the leap to what is seen as traditional. Some see Mind the Gap as their church now, others have chosen to also be involved in Sunday worship at some of the newer churches in the area. We are learning that it is the kingdom that is important.'

We are learning that it is the kingdom that is important

The leaders of Mind the Gap recognise that any new ministry such as this cannot be done whilst also attempting to sustain the current work in a local church. Their circuit was bold enough to release one of their ministers from some pastoral responsibility in order to devote time to this new venture. The team leaders have also had to cut back on some of the things they were doing in order to create time for new things. 'Even cell members are starting to recognise that if all their time is spent doing things in the church, then they do not have the time to devote to relationships with those who are yet to meet Jesus,' says Elaine. 'This is not an easy lesson to learn – it is even harder to implement.'

Just a few years ago a group of churches were looked at the declining trends and committed themselves to doing something about it. The decline has not been reversed yet, but they feel with God's continuing guidance, that anything is possible... absolutely anything!

Norma's Story:

Norma had no church connection and was invited to one of Mind the Gap's first Alpha courses, where she became a Christian. She is now a cell leader.

'I became a follower of Jesus Christ three years ago. I had a drink problem and my home was full of rage and violence – at one stage I thought I had killed my husband. I lost my family to drink.

'Three months after asking Jesus into my life I was controlling my drinking habits; shortly after I was teetotal. I have not had a drink for two and a half years, Jesus saved my life! I have my family back; my home is now filled with love, peace and hope in Jesus who died for us so that we could be free.'

Helen's Story:

Helen also came from a non-church background and was invited onto an Alpha course.

'My Christian walk started three years ago. I was very depressed with an alcohol problem. I cried out to God and he answered my prayer. When I heard and understood the story of the cross and how Jesus died for all the bad things I had done and still do, it was the most significant day of my life. I realised that the love he showed me at the cross was not based on performance. There have been some very difficult times but it's knowing that God (if I let him) is in all things working them out for good. Amen! All glory to our Father.'

For more information visit:
www.mind-the-gap-project.tripod.com

CALLED TO THE BAR

CHURCH	BARNONE, CARDIFF
DENOMINATION	INDEPENDENT
CATEGORY	CONGREGATIONAL PLANT
LOCATION	CITY CENTRE

On a Sunday evening in an upstairs section of the Gower Pub in Cardiff, a group of people can be found who share a common focus – Christianity. Otherwise known as Pubchurch, Barnone is having a significant impact in connecting with those who would find it hard to engage with traditional church.

WHAT IS PUBCHURCH?

Barnone is a community of people trying their best to work out who God is and how knowing him changes they way they live. Through studying and putting into practice the teachings of Jesus Christ, they are committed to providing 'places and opportunities' to allow anyone and everyone to interact with God

A typical Barnone evening will include a live DJ, a singer-songwriter or band, Bibles and newspapers on the tables and a bar that is open throughout the 'service' selling alcohol and soft drinks. The Tab, which is the monthly information magazine with articles, stories and scriptures on the month's theme, is also available.

There will be a ten to fifteen minute chat from the bar by a guest, using personal story and Bible input on the theme of the night, followed by a short prayer at the end of the night to wrap it all up. There will also be a discussion on a given topic as well as time to catch up with friends, meet new people and discuss ideas.

Our aim at Barnone is to plant ourselves back in the heart of a community

The concept was born from the shared vision of Chris Coffey and Bill and Rachel Taylor-Beales who between them co-ordinate the ministry. It is also a congregation and an important part of the larger Glenwood Church, and therefore responsible to its leadership team.

PLACES

Chris, Bill and Rachel are clear about what it is they are trying to do. 'Our aim at Barnone is to plant ourselves back in the heart of a community, to bar none that are looking for answers or a place to ask questions. Pubs by definition are public space, they feel habitable and unpretentious, a quality that, unfortunately, is not shared by many churches.' They go on to say that 'there are many different ways in which we try and interact with the concept and reality of an interventionist God. These include discussion through Bible and issue-based studies, worship through social action and creative meditation and communion through eating and drinking together.'

VALUES

Some of the central values of the Barnone community include:

- Being committed to the welfare of the smaller group of Barnone regulars and the wider community they live in

- Respecting everyone and the 'journey' that they are on

- Being committed to 'meeting and praying together' and making it a priority in their lives

- Looking for ways to be a 'positive experience' for the wider community.

All members of Barnone are invited to contribute what they can to the overall life of the group, on the basis that everyone has something they can offer. Some people come however needing to receive much more than they can give. Chris, Bill and Rachel stress that 'this is a completely legitimate place to be and we are committed to making sure that we provide a safe place for people to sort out their next steps on their journey, whatever those steps are and wherever they are going. We are committed to providing regular "food" in both the emotional and spiritual sense through the teaching, prayer and worship at Barnone.'

. . . a safe place for people to sort out their next steps on their journey

They are keen to point out however that they do not wish to provide or feed into a 'Consumer' mentality which might suggest that anyone coming to Barnone will have all their needs taken care of without them taking some responsibility. 'We are not a club, we are a community, and therefore all of us are responsible and accountable to each other.'

DISCUSSION

At every level of Barnone is the element of discussion; they firmly believe that God is big enough to face some major questions. Sunday evenings will always include discussion and debate as well as an opportunity for anyone to just come along and find out about who and what Pubchurch is all about.

WORSHIP

Worship is an important part of Barnone's life and they emphasise that it takes different forms. 'There is the worship we show through loving our neighbour in the local community and there is also the worship where we engage one on one with God. This is done both privately and corporately, from simple, quiet meditation, walking and praying, to employing the use of the arts such as music, painting, writing and dance.' Once a month, there is an evening of creative worship which gives an opportunity for people to engage both openly and experimentally with God.

We are committed to helping people work out and work through their personal journey of faith

'We are committed to helping people work out and work through their personal journey of faith,' say Chris, Bill and Rachel. 'We are in the process, through alternative sources such as film and literature, of exploring over the next year what it is to be a disciple of Christ and how "discipling" can happen within the Barnone context.'

Pubchurch offers a number of distinct and creative ways to help people explore faith without having to adapt to a traditional church culture. By remaining a congregation of a mother church they have access to resources, support and an accountability structure that might otherwise make this a difficult ministry to maintain.

Ruth's Story:

When I first went to Barnone, I knew nothing about church. Nothing good anyway. I was there almost under protest, following 18 months of arguing with a good friend of mine, Sarah, whom I met in my first year at university. On the very rare occasions she got me to her church, I found the whole experience cringe-worthy and at times upsetting. People waved their hands in the air and prayed out loud. When I was introduced to people after the service I didn't know what to say. I didn't get the in-jokes about the Bible and all I wanted to do was sneak off for a cigarette, even though I thought it would be frowned upon.

Barnone was established sometime during my second year, and it was Sarah who dragged me along. I was still deeply suspicious of all Christians and what I saw as their attempts at 'converting' me, but I went along because, much as I hated to admit it, there was something about all this God stuff which just wouldn't go away.

When we got there I remember squeezing onto a table and worrying that I would have to talk to strangers. I had a pint and then another one and then I started to relax. When Chris, one of the leaders, eventually came over and said he hadn't seen me here before, I was ready to talk. I said how normal it felt to be there, how sometimes I thought I might believe in a God, but how Christianity felt like a whole other world in which I had no place.

On his suggestion, I signed up for the Alpha course there and then. Ten weeks of pints, food and discussions in the pub later, we were on the weekend away in West Wales.

On the Saturday night everyone was praying in a group in the chapel and I felt the Holy Spirit move in me.

The pub church community is just as important to me now, even though I no longer live in Cardiff. It provides me with many things – including straight answers to my endless questions and concerns – but above all it's a place where it feels safe to be vulnerable, to open up and to be myself.

 For more information visit: www.pubchurch.com

RE-BOOTING THE CHURCH

CHURCH	*ST JAMES, CLERKENWELL, LONDON*
DENOMINATION	*CHURCH OF ENGLAND*
CATEGORY	*ESTABLISHED CHURCH – NEW INITIATIVE*
LOCATION	*CITY CENTRE*

St James is a local church right in the heart of London. Since the Middle Ages, Clerkenwell has been a place of protest and free speech just outside London's city walls and the current church continues that tradition of presenting a counter-cultural message to all who will listen.

There has been a church on the site since 1100 but in 1997 the decision was taken to make a new start and the small group of faithful Christians appointed Andrew Baughen with the mandate to re-establish a gospel-focused work for all the people of Clerkenwell – what is called by some a 'church reboot'.

'The starting point was to agree a reason for seeking to build another church in the area,' says Andrew. 'After all it was clear that the residents of the area were already well served by very well known churches almost on the doorstep - from the robed choirs of St Paul's Cathedral or St Bartholemew the Great (the next door parish) through to the first class teaching of St Helen's, Bishopsgate and with plenty in between there was already a church to suit every possible taste. It also became evident that the Christians living in the area were already linked into church and were very resistant to moving to one with only a couple of handfuls of people - "I think it's great what you're doing but for the sake of our children we need to stick with All Souls".'

The church decided there was no point in being a miniature All Souls, St Helen's, Holy Trinity Brompton or Hillsongs, especially when the real thing was only a few minutes down the road. Instead, the vision agreed on was to focus on the thousands of people living in the local area who have never heard of those other churches, but know about St James because they walk by on their way to the tube or can see the church tower from their tower block window. A motto was developed that St James was 'a church reaching the people other churches cannot reach.'

That vision had a major effect on the type of church that was then built. From the outset the services were geared to local people – and that meant all local people. The question to be answered, explains Andrew, was 'How do we communicate with people in the council estates, people who have lived in Clerkenwell for generations, people new to the area living in the loft conversions, students in the local halls of residence, young couples, people new to London, elderly, families, international students, city professionals, cabbies and trades workers – in fact the full smorgasboard of people you find in the centre of a capital city.' The answer was to focus on the issues common to all as raised in the mediums of film, television and music, with answers from the biblical truths. Every sermon or talk therefore sought to explore the Bible's relevance to issues by projecting clips from film or a current TV programme or by making a vox pop interview on the theme. The experience was that mainstream films and TV are common to the majority of people even if their life-stage, experience and cultural identities are very different. People may listen to very different music stations but all watch the latest blockbuster at the movies.

The other way the vision of the church affected the type of congregation that was being built, was that from day one the assumption was there were outsiders present and their needs mattered. Another motto used a lot in planning meetings was 'never assume' – the preaching never assumed that people accepted the basic tenets of the Bible or had any Bible story background. Every week it was expected that there would be people who needed to hear and needed their eyes opening to grace. This meant care was taken over what words were used, which cross references to make and particularly how the passage was applied. 'In fact in the whole service each week,' says Andrew, 'it is still made clear that it is fine to be "just looking".' Each service begins with a 'connecting with God' section, then an 'exploring the theme' section and then a 'responding to the theme' section which includes the majority of the songs, by which time people have learnt why Christians would want to be singing these things to God. St James aims to disarm people, to help them see church which is recognisable but attractively interesting and contemporary.

The vision to build a church for those not used to church is reflected in St James' mission statement 'to build a thirst for God's rescue and a devotion to God's rule.' The statement deliberately points out the 'belief in process' - that coming to faith for many is a long journey with many stages and barriers to overcome on the way. The initial aim of the church therefore is to simply build a thirst for God and his rescue plan - for people to start to see their need of the water of life so they eventually come to the point of drinking and then growing in full devotion. The church's values also reflect the journey of faith - St James seeks to be a place of community, discovery and engagement; all prayer and planning centres on being those three things.

> . . . *coming to faith for many is a long journey with many stages and barriers to overcome on the way*

Having a clear idea of what the church's role is within the panoply of churches in London enables decisions to be made about what is and what isn't necessary to support the vision. The focus therefore is on activities which enable the church to be meeting unchurched local people rather than attracting existing Christians. 'The church has worked hard at opening up its facilities to the local community and being involved in local festivals and events' says Andrew. 'Great care is taken over publicity distributed in the parish so the first impression people have of the church is a good one.' Sundays are also made into a community event each week with breakfast beforehand, top quality coffee afterwards and a free lunch once a month.

'The best thing about St James,' says Andrew, 'is the knowledge that the church is making a difference to the lives of local people in Clerkenwell - now that's a vision worth giving my life to!'

Sue's Story:

I first came to St James when I was new to the area and went along to the 2x2 toddler group with my daughter Sydney to find new friends. Whilst there, I noticed a sign asking for people to help run the crèche on Sundays during the morning service. I applied for the position thinking it would just be another opportunity to meet people in the area. Each Sunday I'd arrive at the church to see people gathering, chatting, drinking coffee, eating croissants and began to feel this tremendous sense of joy and community which I wanted to be a part of. I also became inquisitive about what went on in the services, as I had only ever attended a church service for weddings or funerals, and wondered what it was all about.

A fellow member of St James informed me of the Women's Group Bible studies, held weekly. I was made to feel very welcome when I joined and found it to be both informative and supportive. I wanted to know more and asked if they'd mind if I stopped doing the crèche so I could attend Sunday services. St James makes you feel as if you've always been a part of it, but above all it makes you feel valued. I was introduced to Jesus, found a new friend and my faith came alive.

My knowledge of the Gospels and of Jesus was non-existent so going to the Simply Christianity course helped me understand why Jesus came to save us and how we are forgiven for our sins. In June 2005, my daughter and I were baptised together. St James provides never-ending opportunities for my faith to grow and to be put into practice.

Before I felt like a bird looking for a nest when there aren't many trees around. Since being a member of St James, I feel like I've found my nest.

 For more information visit: www.jc-church.org

LIVING THE MESSAGE

CHURCH	*LIVING HOPE CHURCH, DUDLEY*
DENOMINATION	*INDEPENDENT*
CATEGORY	*NEW CHURCH PLANT*
LOCATION	*SUBURBAN*

'Why not have a go at running a church in here?' was the surprising challenge to Pastor Jeremy Parkes. Surprising because it came from the head of Milking Bank Estate's school in Dudley, the only community building on the 2,000 home development. Jeremy said, 'I knew it was a word from God, like Paul's call to help from the man of Macedonia.'

Today that church has grown five-fold, and is near bursting point.

After time spent carefully and prayerfully formulating and teaching the new church's central values with the core group, great care was also given to preparing the local community for the launch of the congregation. Jeremy and his wife Joy visited every home on the estate. 'This was very productive, and people remember the visit, often with a fondness that surprises us,' comments Jeremy. 'I believe it's so important to befriend the community and have a vision of what you will become.'

A group of 30 Christians and five children, who met to prepare the church launch at the Ward Arms Hotel, Dudley, has now swelled to a congregation of 120 adults and 35 children, filling the school hall.

It's so important to befriend the community and have a vision of what you will become

Dudley in the West Midlands is a diverse community, including several more prosperous areas, compared with some parts of the Black Country.

Self-employed and professionals figure highly on those living on Milking Bank, as well as commuters to the nearby cities of Wolverhampton and Birmingham.

'Their needs may not be obvious to the casual observer,' says Jeremy, 'but a closer look shows "pinch points" on issues from relationships to redundancy, where God's support is extremely welcome.'

They grow by seeing God at work

An important value for the church is to encourage those who are attending but who are not yet Christians, to become stewards, to greet visitors, or to join overseas missions. Experienced Christians give them support. 'They grow by seeing God at work and this approach to evangelism wipes away a "them and us" attitude,' says Jeremy.

Worship and inspiration are the priorities on Sundays. Through the week, life change and friendship are important and are fostered in small groups, Bible-reading groups and prayer teams. Every theme that is taught in the church is also discussed and questioned 'Alpha-style' in small groups – this is where friendships grow, care is given and disciples are made.

Mission is central to Living Hope, which has interests abroad and at home, its members devoting time and effort to helping those in Ukraine, Albania and Zimbabwe find Christ. 'This wider approach recognises that local activity is only a part and seeing the bigger picture encourages healthy growth,' says Jeremy.

So what has been learnt through this church planting experience? 'The positive difference for me' says Jeremy 'is that we believe our community wants us here. I've had a mind-shift change. I once thought that people did not want to listen but they're waiting to hear from us.'

Liz's Story:

Liz had a church upbringing but moved away in her mid teens as she could not reconcile the way she was living with the expectations and ideals placed upon her. She said she found the church unforgiving, which made it difficult to grow up in a normal teenage way.

She spent the following seven years without any real spiritual input, until being invited to join an Alpha course, at what happened to be the worst time of her life. A lot of bad things had happened and she had no real way of coping.

She said: 'Bad things were all stacked up on top of each other. I remember Jeremy asked me how my partner was and I cried because I was so vulnerable, I didn't think I could open up. But I decided to stick it out, as things couldn't get any worse. It was then that I had a dramatic pick-up: I realised that I did not feel rubbish all the time. Other people started noticing something different. Coming back to God didn't change my problems but it gave me a new way of dealing with them. My sister was clinically depressed and she joined me at Alpha. She is now happy, with a baby. I didn't actually want any of it. I didn't want any involvement with church because of the problems earlier. But once in it, I couldn't resist it. I have been coming for 12 months now and it is part of my life.'

 For more information visit: www.livinghopechurch.org.uk

CHURCH WITH NO NAME

CHURCH	*CABLE STREET COMMUNITY CHURCH, SHADWELL, LONDON*
DENOMINATION	*BAPTIST/URBAN EXPRESSION*
CATEGORY	*NEW CHURCH PLANT*
LOCATION	*URBAN*

Parties, BBQs and a holiday to Butlins are just some of the methods used by Cable Street Community Church to help them connect with the people in Shadwell, Tower Hamlets.

A team led by Jim and Juliet Kilpin all moved into the local estates with the express purpose of becoming part of the community. 'We wanted to become part of the community and experience all the joys and hardships of living in this inner-city neighbourhood,' explains Juliet. 'We recognised that many people in urban areas were fed up of well-meaning Christians commuting in from nicer parts of the suburbs, so to win respect we felt that we needed to move into the area.'

Although in essence the team (who were from Urban Expression, an urban mission agency), were being church with one another from day one, they didn't advertise services or even give it a name until some time later. A couple of local men became Christians and told them they were finding it difficult to explain to their friends what they were part of. They asked if the church could have a name, so they were encouraged to think of one themselves. They came up with Cable Street Community Church. 'In this way,' explains Juliet, 'the church was born out of the community, rather than being something that was seen to be imposed upon it. We wanted church to grow naturally and allow those who became Christians to shape what it would become. We felt that urban church planting was in effect cross-cultural mission just as much as those involved in work overseas.'

> We felt that urban church planting was in effect cross-cultural mission

From the start there was a commitment to meeting in homes as it was felt that this was where some aspects of being church happened best. 'Deeper relationships are built over the intimacy of a meal, problems are more likely to be shared and worship is more likely to be multi-voiced,' says Juliet. The fact that they had no building of their own gave strength to this approach, although they say they were definitely not hankering after their own premises. Today, eight years on, they still meet in homes on Sundays for Estate Church, an informal gathering of people from each of the distinct neighbourhoods. Each Estate Church has Estate Pastors who intentionally live 'on-site' and seek the well-being of the community.

A few years after starting, the leaders noticed that for some people a meeting in a home was too intimate, and so they began to meet midweek in a local church hall, which despite its name was still viewed as quite a neutral venue. Still wanting to maintain a non-churchy, informal style, they chose to still eat together and were careful not to call it a service. Teaching evenings are known as 'Taking Root' and once a month there is 'Sacred Space' where the church sanctuary is used for a labyrinth-style quiet, contemplative prayer evening. The church also has occasional Art Zones and joint worship celebrations. The hall belongs to a high Anglo-Catholic church with whom Cable Street Community Church have developed a surprisingly close partnership, even employing a youth worker together. The blend of historical and traditional spirituality with the informality and mission focus of Cable Street Community Church seems to work very well.

Outreach has always been focused on going to people rather than expecting people to come to them. Juliet believes that not having a building to invite people to, helped with this approach! Practical service, sports programmes, detached youth work and helping with youth clubs run by other agencies have all played their part. The church has also helped with the regeneration of a local adventure playground.

'Although the number of people who gather for worship is currently between twenty and thirty, those who feel that we are their church is probably nearer 100,' says Juliet. 'Many of these people are

Many of these people are certainly on a journey with Jesus

certainly on a journey with Jesus, but they have started from a long way back, and discipling people who don't enjoy coming to meetings, is always a challenge!'

The church has seen people saved from a drug background and celebrated their stories but there has also been heartbreak when others have fallen away or got drawn back into their old lifestyle. 'The

> It is not so much that they have lost their faith and rejected church, but are recovering from the fact that church has rejected them

movement of people away from the locality for a variety of reasons has often caused things to become fragile again, having just felt stable for a short while,' says Juliet. 'Some of the local community have found a spiritual home with us after being rejected by other churches because of their behaviour or appearance. It is not so much that they have lost their faith and rejected church, but are recovering from the fact that church has rejected them.'

Raising local people into leadership has been a challenge, in part this is because some are starting such a long way back in terms of faith. 'It may have something to do with the high levels of mental health problems exhibited locally too,' explains Juliet. 'This is often as a result of living in inner-city locations and being powerless to change their own circumstances, which means that people's confidence is sometimes fragile and their reliability and stability is challenged.'

Jim and Juliet are not confident that this expression of church will ever be 'strong' or 'successful' in terms of average church statistics, but it is reaching people that other churches often avoid and is challenging the trend of Christians moving out of urban environments, which they believe in an increasing urban environment cannot be a bad thing.

Freddy's Story:

I first went to Cable Street Community Church about seven years ago. I met Jim and Juliet before I ever set foot inside the church, or should I say house, because at that time the church was meeting in two different homes. To me this was a very comfortable way to go to church, as just going into a church building would have been a massive step. Over the years I have struggled with an addiction to drugs, but church has always been there for me.

The main thing about Cable Street Community Church is what it says – community. All are welcome, but the make up of the church is local. Even some people who move away still have a connection with the local area and come back for church.

The ministers and leaders are of a young average age, all in their twenties or thirties. This isn't to say that older people do not bring wisdom, but having young leadership means that things can change and adapt quickly when needed. Over the last seven years the biggest change I have seen is in the young people. Many who I would have labelled as being pregnant, or drug addicts, or in prison by the age of sixteen, and overdosed at the age of twenty, are now blossoming into young energetic, ambitious adults – which is great.

Cymone's Story:

I started attending Cable Street Community Church about a year ago. My first impression was that it felt like a social gathering where there was no religion, just a strong belief in God. This was what made me happy and so I decided to attend regularly with my daughter and we both enjoy it very much.

I don't really believe in following a religion, I just believe in God and when I'm at church I feel I can be myself and I don't feel like I'm being pressured into anything.

Overall I'm glad I joined because now I have also gained a great extended family.

 For more information on Urban Expression visit: www.urbanexpression.org.uk

AMAZING GRACE

CHURCH	*GRACE CHRISTIAN FELLOWSHIP, CORK*
DENOMINATION	*INDEPENDENT*
CATEGORY	*NEW CHURCH PLANT*
LOCATION	*SUBURBAN*

Grace Christian Fellowship is passionate about being an Irish church. It is eager to tear down all the cultural walls of division that have up to now existed between the average Irish people in the street and a local evangelical church. 'Historically,' says Pastor Tom Burke, 'any Bible-based, non-Catholic church in the Republic of Ireland has tended to reflect the national culture of the missionary who founded it, usually American or English.'

Grace is a non-denominational church based in the inner suburbs of Cork, on the south coast of Ireland. Beginning as a small group of 11 friends gathering together in a home in December 1996, it now meets in a large school hall with a total congregation of just under four hundred.

With a mission statement called the '3 R's', standing for Relationship, Reachout and Relevant, the church is committed to applying biblical principles to the context of modern Irish culture.

We allow people to belong before they believe

'One of our deepest values is to be a community that allows searchers time to travel their faith journey while feeling a sense of belonging' says Tom. 'In essence, we allow people to belong before they believe and in almost all cases they do follow on to believe. Irish people tend to be emotional, not very reserved with stiff upper lips or anything like that. So it's very important to be demonstrative, it's so important to have an atmosphere where people can sense that they are loved and accepted.

'We don't really do any outreach at all,' he goes on. 'We do have parties though, such as the *Ceilidhi* (Irish Dances) and some come along to church through those, but mainly it's friendship evangelism.' The majority of those coming to Grace do so from a practising Catholic background and so in a sense, much of the church's growth is from prodigals. Over the last nine years about two hundred people who would fit into this category have been baptised. 'We were almost all at one time practising Catholics,' comments Tom, 'many of us took our faith very seriously but became disillusioned along the way. There was usually a good foundation of Bible stories from childhood along with a moral code of living. However what we lacked was that personal relationship with Jesus as a friend, rather than just following rules and regulations. There is a huge spiritual void appearing in Irish life and most unbelievers will know and sense it's there and that it's in them.'

The church has found it necessary to change some of their practices to accommodate those who are seeking. One of which is the form used for communion. They realised that passing bread and wine from person to person, row to row was an unnecessary cultural barrier to those who were used to going forward at the Mass, so the communion service was recently changed to reflect more sensitively what was familiar to local people. Communion is now served from the front of the church and has been a great success both for members and seekers.

Each new believer is personally encouraged to get involved in the life of the church community as soon as they feel comfortable to do so. 'We have found it works best if one of the more mature or experienced church members comes alongside and befriends them, so starting a one-to-one friendship,' says Tom. 'This is often inbuilt anyway, as it's usually through personal friendship that the new person comes along in the first place. It seems one-to-one works best in our situation, probably because we can adapt to each individual need.'

Despite some being upset at Grace's way of doing church, Tom points out that the fruit was very evident right from the beginning, with converts and prodigals becoming disciples but admits that it took a while to fully disengage from their critics and really run at full speed.

The best thing? 'It has to be seeing lost and disillusioned souls getting right with God, coming back to the One who loves them, finding peace after all the wandering, and somehow, for reasons beyond our comprehension, God choosing in part to use us to accomplish this.'

Colin's Story:

Colin is typical of what the Lord has done with so many lives at Grace Fellowship. Growing up in the suburbs of Cork city, like most he was brought up as a Catholic and learned about God the Father, Son and Holy Spirit. This left a strong foundation in Colin of a general belief in Jesus and that somehow the Bible contained knowledge about God and how to live a good life. But again, like most young Irish people, Colin began to fall away from the Catholic Church during his teens.

He drifted into a lifestyle of heavy drinking, which increased even more after he started work as an apprentice plasterer. Along with this lifestyle came the hard man image of wine, women and song. But all was not well in Colin's heart. Feeling depressed and empty, at twenty-four the world should have been his oyster, but instead, for Colin it began to look increasingly bleak and meaningless. It was at this point that he began to look for spiritual answers. His search eventually led him to start talking to some other lads who he met through a workmate. Some of these were members of Grace Fellowship.

Colin prayed with his new friends asking Jesus to forgive him, and then came to church for the first time the following Sunday. Because the meeting was in a Catholic school hall he felt this new type of church couldn't be too far out, or else the religious order who ran the school wouldn't have allowed them to meet there. His first impression was the warm welcome he received from so many during the pre-service coffee time. When there was a word shared during the meeting about someone with a specific need, Colin knew this was God speaking to him. So, in front of hundreds of people, he walked up to the front for prayer, answering the call to receive a healing touch from God.

He liked the worship which was lively and he also found that he could relate to the preaching style and loved that it was OK to laugh out loud at the jokes. Everyone there was dressed casually just like him, most people were local just like him and most had come from a Catholic background – just like him. It was new and strange but comfortable and almost familiar at the same time.

Colin began to make a lot of friends his own age at Grace and started hanging out with them. Six months later he wanted to get baptised in water and joined 18 others in the Atlantic Ocean at the Cork coast on a sunny Saturday in April. Nearly one year on, Colin's life has changed deeply. The depression is nothing compared to what it was, he never seems to miss church on Sundays or during the week and his mother has also just started attending the church with him. He has good days and not so good days, but he has never been anywhere near as low as he used to be before Jesus came into his life.

 For more information visit: www.graceireland.com

A HEART FOR MISSION

CHURCH	*C3, CAMBRIDGE*
DENOMINATION	*INDEPENDENT*
CATEGORY	*NEW CHURCH PLANT*
LOCATION	*CITY-WIDE*

A charismatic evangelical church in Cambridge, C3 started over twenty years ago with a handful of families meeting in a home. Since then it has moved venue a number of times in order to accommodate its growth. Today the congregation is made up of mainly young professionals and families with a membership of about four hundred and fifty adults and children.

A mission statement of 'reaching and shaping a generation with the message and cause of Christ' is undergirded by three principle values:

Being

- Christ Centred
- Purpose Driven
- People Empowering

'We are committed to being a church for the unchurched and to helping people become mature believers,' says Steve Campbell, senior pastor. 'We are also passionate about the church. We believe that she is the hope of the world as she carries the message of the kingdom.

'Sunday meetings have always taken a lot of work,' he goes on, 'and we realised that wasn't going to change any time soon, so we decided that we should use Sundays to be a major connection point with the unchurched.'

The leaders asked why people were not bringing their friends and family members to the meetings and came up with two answers:

- People were not connecting with unsaved people.
- They were embarrassed to bring them to church as too many cringy things went on that Christians grow accustomed to and excuse, but the unchurched are not so tolerant.

The church set about training people to reach their friends and then encouraged them to bring a guest to the Sunday meetings which were specially designed to be made accessible and excellent. They aimed to create a safe environment to hear a very unsafe message.

'There's no doubt that the greatest change that was needed in the church has not been a structural one but a heart issue,' says Steve. 'Knowing lost people really matter to God and feeling God's heartbeat for them has been the biggest change. When you feel this you'll change anything and not complain.'

. . . the church has not been a structural one but a heart issue

Steve goes on to say that the biggest practical change has been in relation to the Sunday services. 'We took time to teach that "church is so not about me" and that we exist for mission. We wanted everyone to be looking outward and this was to include the Sunday service.'

As a result, the Sunday meetings became a lot shorter and they changed some of the ways that they worshipped so that visitors would feel included. 'We agreed to limit our liberty in that context for the sake of the visitor or uninitiated,' explains Steve. 'We still saw our Sundays as church but it became "church with manners" rather than self-indulgent.' The church also began to explore using a greater variety of media. They recognised that people live in a visual age, so now all the announcements are via a big screen and a lot more media is used in the preaching.

Making guests feel welcome without being overwhelmed has been important as has the commitment to allowing visitors to remain anonymous if they so desire.

In all they do C3 has aimed to raise the bar of excellence. 'We try to get rid of the "This is good enough for church" mentality and aim for excellence,' says Steve. 'Why? Because it glorifies God but also because it attracts the unbeliever. We know God looks on the heart but we cannot escape the fact that man looks on the outward appearance. Many people don't give God a chance because the outward appearance of the church puts them off listening to the message.'

Clinton's Story:

Although I've believed in God all my life, it wasn't until 2004 that I was reborn. It was at C3 church in Cambridge at a time when I felt something missing in my life and a longing to know Jesus Christ and become like him.

The first time I went to a Sunday meeting it was so comfortable and enjoyable, and the music so passionate. I know if I hadn't enjoyed church so much that Sunday, I probably would never have returned. The previous week my parents had sent me a book I had never heard of called *The Purpose Driven Life* by Rick Warren (Zondervan, 2002). That first week I went to church, C3 were beginning the 40 days of purpose. For the first time I started reading the Bible and found it suddenly to be fascinating and the small group I attended really helped me grow.

It's still a daily struggle but I know I am slowly changing.

There are times when I need to apologise to someone, and previously I would have just let it pass, whereas now I sense a conviction and lack of peace until I make things right.

I have found too that when I seriously try to get closer to God countless distractions block the path, and I often feel guilty when I fail. I still find it hard to believe that Jesus loves me unconditionally but I know that I'm on my way.

It was at C3 that I was baptised, and I'm so glad now that I went through with it. I've learnt so much from God. He is good no matter what happens in life.

Discipleship is developed through small groups. Everyone is encouraged to be involved and an 'in house' curriculum along with a DVD is provided to all the group leaders. When someone becomes a Christian they are assigned to a small group and someone is allocated to mentor the new convert by going through a special DVD series called 'Shaping a Generation'.

if you can get the heart right, much else will take care of itself!

Steve reflects that if he did this again he would go a little slower. 'For some people we probably made the changes too quickly and it perhaps unnecessarily frightened them. As a result some bolted!' but he strongly believes that 'if you can get the heart right, much else will take care of itself! Methods come and go but God's heart for the lost remains constant.' And the best thing of

Oh for so much more of this!

all? 'Seeing people who were once unbelievers become followers of Christ and carry it through. Oh for so much more of this!'

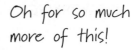 *For more information visit:* www.cthree.org

NET-WORKING

CHURCH	*THE NET, HUDDERSFIELD*
DENOMINATION	*ANGLICAN*
CATEGORY	*NETWORK CHURCH PLANT*
LOCATION	*TOWN CENTRE*

Frustrated with the cultural gap between church and unchurched people, Dave Male, an Anglican minister, decided to have a conversation with his local bishop.

What eventually followed were plans for a new church and The Net was formally launched in 1999 as a church to reach unchurched people in Huddersfield.

Dave explains that 'Discovering Willow Creek Church was an important landmark, as was beginning a monthly seeker-style service in a local pub in Huddersfield in 1996.' It took two years for permission to be given from the diocesan authorities and initially it began with Dave, his wife Heather and their three children. Nine months later about four hundred local Christians came to support the official opening of the church.

The driving force has always been mission

'The driving force has always been mission,' says Dave. 'Surveys suggested that at least 55 per cent of people in Huddersfield had no contact with any church. This was the group that The Net wanted to reach and connect with. There was also a realisation that in a mobile society the geographical confines of a parish were too limiting, and so it was decided to try and work through our networks of relationships.'

Starting with 28 adults and 12 children, they initially just met on a Tuesday evening where they hammered out key values and a mission statement: 'By knowing and loving God and each other we seek to enable unchurched people to develop a real and relevant relationship with Jesus.' This statement has continued to be the motivating force for the church.

'A lot of emphasis has been put on developing a network of good relationships with non-Christian family, friends and workmates,' says Dave. 'We try to minimise meetings and maximise relationships by regularly having social and seeker events to bring friends along to. These are usually held on a Friday or Saturday night and often use multimedia presentations to cover every type of topic from chocolate to suffering and from sport to *The Da Vinci Code*. Other networks have developed around special interest groups such as sport, parenting, marriage, the internet, through the church's website and work. These have brought the church into contact with people beyond the normal friendship circles of the members. Dave says that some of the highlights of using this strategy include an annual football coaching course for children and youth that regularly attracts over one hundred, none of whom have any church contact; a relationship course run in a local gym for the gym members and the website which has been having over ten thousand hits a month. This style of networking means that people come to the church from all over Huddersfield and from the surrounding area.

This mission imperative has meant that The Net has no buildings of its own and no plans exist for obtaining one. A variety of venues have been used for corporate worship including an art gallery, the university, a hotel and currently a high school. Outreach events are held at locations that fit in with what the church is trying to achieve and these have included a restaurant, a function room at Huddersfield Town Football Club, a sports bar and hotel facilities. Although setting up in different locations can be tiresome, the church finds it releasing not to be tied to a building or to its financial implications.

About a hundred people now attend the church, including children, youth and adults. Most of the adults are aged between eighteen to fifty and many of these have come to faith as part of The Net. Dave says, 'We make it plain on our website that we don't really encourage people to leave their churches in Huddersfield to join us. We don't want to be growing through transfers.'

As well as mission being important, relationships are undoubtedly key for The Net. 'We have done a lot of work on developing our relationships and discovering how God has made us relational beings,' says Dave. 'We often use Genesis 2:18 – "It is not good for the man to be alone", as a reminder of God's provision for relationships and not just marriage. An important element of this has been our small groups. We started using the cell group system but recently felt they were not really helping us to fulfil our mission statement. Last April we changed them dramatically and now have six interest type groups which include a Bible study group, a young adults group, a social action group and a running group.'

Children and youth have always been important elements of the church's life. It was made clear from the start that the mission statement and values were for all ages and not just the adults. A children's worker was employed right from the beginning of the church and more recently they have taken on a full-time youth worker, both supported through church giving.

We often feel we have more questions than answers

'It's not always been plain sailing,' stresses Dave. 'We often feel we have more questions than answers. We are still trying to grapple with how to connect with ordinary people in the Huddersfield area who have no contact with any church but have spiritual questions.'

'When we started,' Dave continues, 'people were asked what they were most excited about and most fearful of. Almost everyone answered the same, it was beginning with a blank piece of paper – it is so exciting but also very scary. Good job we trust in a great God.'

Angela's Story:

Angela is a college lecturer in nursing. Her neighbours, Debbie and Jeff invited her to The Net's carol service at the George Hotel. 'It was funny; they used media clips, it made me laugh,' says Angela.

She attended a few of the university hall meetings and found them non-threatening. 'I didn't feel judged or pressurised and didn't feel that the person at the front was controlling.' She signed up for a 'Just Looking' course. 'It was eight weeks looking at faith in depth and I met others like me.' She was impressed that church people she didn't know invited her and her husband to lunch.

Robin Gamble came to preach and invited those who felt they believed in Jesus to stand. She felt herself hovering on the chair but unable to stand. The next week, she asked if she could say something at the end of the service. She said, 'I want to be one of you. This is the path I have chosen.'

Her declaration prompted three others to become Christians after the service. The effervescence with which Angela tells her story is accompanied by the acknowledgement that this has been a long road, 'With hindsight, I had been looking for a long time.'

She recalls nine years earlier when she and Heather Male met by chance as two very pregnant mums who caught one another's eyes, laughed and commiserated together, before walking separate ways. Now she knows that Heather prayed for her that day.

 For more information visit: www.netchurch.org.uk

EDINBURGH'S OFFICE BLOCK PARISH

CHURCH	*ST CUTHBERT'S, EDINBURGH*
DENOMINATION	*CHURCH OF SCOTLAND*
CATEGORY	*ESTABLISHED CHURCH – NEW INITIATIVE*
LOCATION	*CITY CENTRE*

There is an oasis at the heart of Edinburgh's financial services sector, one that reaches out to and serves the businesses, government agencies, hotels and theatres around Lothian Road in Edinburgh's West End.

The brainchild of the parish church of St Cuthbert's, situated midway between Lothian Road and West Princes Street Gardens, OASIS was conceived in the nineties. The church began to consider how it could serve the office workers who were beginning to fill the new buildings in the area and who were becoming the 'new parishioners'. The vision was to start an outreach, with the support and endorsement of other local churches, which would offer a supportive Christian presence to people working in the area. Iain Archibald, Consultant to OASIS explains that it functions a bit like a department store with four different levels.

It is a way of letting people know that we exist and care

'On the ground floor,' says Iain, 'OASIS lays on community-building events of a fun nature. At these, office workers get to know folk in the businesses nearby, it is a way of letting people know that we exist and care.' Organising events such as an Inter-Office Quiz Night or an Inter-Office Relay Race and Fun Run in Princes Street Gardens has produced an excellent response.

Up on the second level, OASIS also offers lunchtime talks on subjects relevant to business people by addressing issues of concern which may not be covered by in-house training courses. 'A recent subject was entitled: "How do I help a colleague, client, friend or relative who is suffering from depression?"' says Iain. 'We like to host these talks in local offices and invite people to come from all round the area. They start with sandwiches and a chat and then the expert, who gives their services freely, speaks for 30 minutes. Some guests chalk up attendance at OASIS lunchtimes in their Continuing Professional Development (CPD) record.'

Further up the escalator, on the third level, is what is known as 'the listening ear'. Fronted by Fiona Hutchison, the associate minister of St Cuthbert's, this is a service that is open to all. Fiona says: 'I am available to meet anyone, of all faiths or none, who may have problems at work or home, and who might feel more comfortable talking things over in confidence with someone not directly involved in their workplace.'

Finally, at the top of the building is 'spiritual exploration'. OASIS offers a Lent course and also a variant of Alpha. This has been pioneered as a lunchtime version for busy office people, under the name of Business Alpha Edinburgh (BAE). Over two hundred guests have gone through the course thus far.

Office workers may dip in and out of any or all the levels. Some only come to the community building events; others take advantage of the listening ear service. A good number start off on the ground floor and work their way right up to the top of the building. 'The people who use OASIS' services are both churched and unchurched,' says Iain. 'People with a church connection tend to form the informal core community within the whole network.'

Originally all the events were held in the church. However, it was soon felt that the spiritual and cultural gap between church and many younger Scots was too wide with too few unchurched people finding their way into the building. It was felt to be a significant move when the OASIS project transitioned into the heart of the world they were trying to serve. Virtually all the communication with those they are seeking to reach is done electronically via email and the website.

Iain sees the development of Business Alpha as a key in OASIS' success and explains that all the talks take place in a local hotel *The Business Alpha course has been life changing* with speakers coming from the business community such as lawyers, accountants, IT and marketing managers. All the talks draw on experience and imagery from the workplace which results in a cringe factor that is next to nothing.

Through this programme, OASIS has seen people returning week after week to meet with their peers and chat about the big issues in life and their world of work. 'This is a place where everyone moves on in their faith journey,' says Iain.

What do the visitors say?

'I found Business Alpha to be a fantastic tool with which I was able to explore and investigate the many questions I had about the Christian faith. I always felt I could ask any questions I wanted and my hosts never made me feel that I might be condemned or belittled for asking either stupid or difficult questions. It has been a very positive experience from beginning to end and I actively looked forward to every Thursday lunchtime for the talk, the chat, the questions and the discussions. Even if I hadn't been interested in Christianity, it would still have been enjoyable just for the chance to have an open and intelligent discussion over lunch!'

'The Business Alpha course has been life changing. It offered me the chance to hear about Christianity and the Bible on an informal, invitational basis. The format is particularly appealing for someone at work with limited time to attend an evening course, each session lasts no more than a lunchtime and can therefore be taken within "office hours".'

'Your organisation (OASIS) is well-named because the weekly talks and discussions afterwards began to seem like an oasis in the desert of the working week! The more I listened, learned and discussed about God, Christ and the Holy Spirit, the more I wanted to find out. This has led to a real deepening of my faith.'

 For more information: visit: www.oasisedinburgh.com

CATCHING THE RHYTHM

CHURCH	NEWSONG COMMUNITY CHURCH, BROMSGROVE
DENOMINATION	INDEPENDENT
CATEGORY	ESTABLISHED CHURCH – NEW INITIATIVE
LOCATION	TOWN CENTRE

'This church is constantly changing. I regularly tell people, if you are looking for a church that stays the same – don't come!' So says Peter Billingham, pastor of NewSong Community Church in Bromsgrove. 'What makes the church unique is that we enjoy discovering the unknown and unexpected, regularly reviewing and adapting all that we are doing.'

Sofas and coffee tables have recently been added to change the feel of the sanctuary for midweek events and a huge array of creative ideas are used to engage with the surrounding community, ranging from 'Baby Bistro' for breastfeeding mums to 'Heartbeat', a local community newspaper with a circulation of 2,500. This is a church that is passionate about using the Arts to communicate the message of the gospel but that equally fervently believes in the importance of building individual, one-to-one relationships. But it hasn't always been this way.

This church is constantly changing

The church as it is today started on 11 November 2000. After a number of years as a very traditional evangelical church it was decided to begin something new. 'Rhythms of Life' was created as a Sunday morning event specifically geared towards the unchurched and over the last few years a style has developed that the church believes is unique, where no two weeks are the same.

Sunday mornings are designed to be church in the twenty-first century. Thoughtful, inspirational worship, drama and multimedia, coupled with practical, Bible-based teaching make this an event for everyone wanting to get some rhythm into their lives and to grow their relationship with God. This is a programme that prioritises those who are not yet believers. It aims to be relaxing, enjoyable and friendly but also addresses real life issues from a clear biblical perspective.

'Alongside all this,' explains Peter, 'we have been experimenting with a number of ways to disciple believers using a Saturday worship service and we have recently launched Thrive, a midweek single site, multi-venue event. Here people gather together for worship, communion and prayer and they have a number of choices for teaching or other options of discipleship.'

With a mission statement of 'to know Jesus more and for more to know Jesus', a common theme that has run through the church since its inception is the metaphor of 'Journey'. 'We understand discipleship as a process,' says Peter 'and being a church that has seen growth through conversions of unchurched people, the challenge is to have patience as the "journey," takes place. We dream of a day when the church will be full of people who know Jesus, not just with head knowledge but with heart and life experiential understanding. We long for a time when significant growth in numbers will come through people discovering Jesus as the source of life.'

NewSong operates a discipling process called 'Running the Race'. 'In the New Testament, the Christian life is often described as a "race to be run",' says Peter, who quotes Hebrews 12.1: 'Therefore . . . let us run with perseverance the race marked out for us' (NIV). 'We are committed to helping followers of Jesus run this race and equipping them to reach greater potential as Christians. We visualise the race as a 400m athletics track, with four distinctive sections to go around. Once 'runners' have gone around the circuit, they are encouraged to help others to run the race, by running with them next time around.'

HOW THE PROGRAMME WORKS

100 STARTING OUT

An introduction to what it means to be a disciple of Jesus Christ, and how to affirm being a part of NewSong Community Church.

200 RUNNING FOR MATURITY

How to improve your prayer life, as well as help in learning other skills, that are marks of a growing disciple. A two hour introductory seminar is followed by a daily reading plan with a weekly discussion group. The course concludes with a one hour session.

300 RUNNING FOR MINISTRY

Discover how to use your SHAPE for Christian Service and Ministry. An eight part seminar course delivered in a small group setting. (SHAPE: Spiritual Gifts, Heart, Abilities, Personality and Experience)

400 RUNNING FOR MISSION

A course helping disciples to become Contagious Christians, using their personal evangelistic style.

When asked what he would do if he did this again, Peter responded by saying: 'I don't know if I would! The process of transitioning a church, as opposed to planting a new one, is very difficult and not to be started unless people are willing to commit for the long haul and are fully aware of the difficulties. The best thing of all though is witnessing the change in people's lives. There is nothing like seeing someone meet Jesus, give their life to him and begin that journey of a lifetime!

The process of transitioning a church, is very difficult

Two Personal Stories:

'Invited to NewSong Community Church by my sister, I walked through the doors on my first visit filled with apprehension and uncertainty. I was suffering from the physical effects of addiction to alcohol over many years and this was a pivotal time in my life. When I walked through the door the warmth and the welcome was apparent in many ways. That day at "Rhythms of Life" there was a "my story" slot with someone telling the story of their life so far as a Christian. I heard how Jesus can change lives and I wanted him to change mine. That day I gave my life to Jesus and never looked back. My greatest joy now is not just that I am free of my addictions, through as each day passes I am increasingly grateful to God – my greatest joy is sharing my story with others. Jesus is still in the business of changing lives, I know, he changed mine.'

'After being a Christian and part of church for most of my life I started coming to NewSong Community Church about eighteen months ago. Apart from the warmth and friendliness of the people and the inspirational quality of the worship, it's the depth of the teaching relevant to everyday life that has had such a huge impact upon me. On only the second visit to NewSong, God challenged me through a message that Pete gave on forgiveness. During the message he said that we need to try to find ways to build bridges in broken relationships. Both my husband and I knew there was a couple we had to call as soon as we got home. The great news is that the bridge was built and what was broken was restored. Being around NewSong has shown me how relevant faith can be to my normal everyday life and it's made all the difference.'

 For more information visit: www.newsong.co.uk

GOD'S REIGN IN SPAIN

CHURCH	MOUNTAINVIEW INTERNATIONAL CHURCH, MADRID
DENOMINATION	INDEPENDENT
CATEGORY	NEW CHURCH PLANT
LOCATION	CITY CENTRE

About one hundred thousand English speaking internationals are living in Madrid and of these less than 1000 (1 per cent) would have any meaningful relationship with Christ. Unlike the Parable of the Lost Sheep, where the Shepherd leaves the 99 to look for the one, Mountainview International Church feels called to leave the one and look for the 99!

Established in March 2002 by Christian Associates International, Mountainview uses natural bridges of friendship, that develop easily in the English language subculture of Madrid, to foster opportunities for dialogue about faith. They have found that, generally speaking, English speakers in the city are looking for opportunities to connect with other English speakers.

The church has grown from two families into a congregation of about seventy-five. There is a strong emphasis on small groups as well as a monthly service in the NW suburbs and a monthly gathering for the groups in the city. The church has developed, somewhat unexpectedly, into two quite distinctive subgroups with very different needs. The city centre is largely characterised by students, other young singles and married couples while in the NW suburbs it is attracting mainly families with children.

Soon it is planned to multiply the church into two congregations so that they will be able to focus more fully on their subgroups.

Church leader Richard Wallace says, 'Our vision is to establish a vital church in Madrid that is radically devoted to God, relentlessly committed to *relentlessly committed to authentic community* authentic community and remarkably passionate for lost people. We seek to be a missional church and take seriously God's call to reach the unchurched millions in Europe.'

Much of Mountainview's time is spent in networking, meeting people and developing relationships. This might be as simple as running a BBQ for a couple of families, or as grandiose as a Guy Fawkes Night which attracted 100 people last year. The aim of these events is simply to provide an opportunity to deepen friendships and demonstrate that people in the church are normal too.

Richard stresses that they usually wait for people to ask them about faith. 'Our experience is that when trust is built up even the most hardened will open up and talk about important issues of life.' They have discovered that in their context friendships need to be fairly deep and significant before people are prepared to talk honestly and openly about spiritual things. Inviting friends to Alpha or a café service is one way that the church seeks to help people explore faith further. Richard's wife Riekje started a Mums and Toddlers group that has nearly fifty mums listed in its directory. She's found this to be a great way to meet people in the community and from the group several mums asked her to start a Bible study group. Richard and Riekje believe it is imperative that others in the church are envisioned to do the same, as they are aware that none of them has the time and resources to sustain more than a handful of significant relationships. Everyone in the church is encouraged to develop three significant friendships with unchurched people.

. . . they still wonder deep down if they are a "project"!

'One of the tensions we have noticed in our networking,' reflects Richard, 'is that even when we become close friends with unchurched people, and even though we hardly push our message at all, they still wonder deep down if they are a "project"! So we need to assure people we reach out to regularly that they are not just an "assignment" but people that we love and care about dearly.'

'We've seen hundreds of people develop a more positive attitude about the church, we've seen dozens open up and talk about matters of faith, we've seen a handful seriously consider faith and we've seen a small number accept Christ.' Richard is very aware of the frustrations of working in an international context such as this and says: 'I wish that things went faster in Europe, but they don't, and so we remind ourselves regularly that although we sow and water, it is God that makes faith grow and that we will be rewarded for our "labour" not our "success" (1 Cor. 3:6-9).

'For me,' he goes on, 'the highlights are when a lady my wife has been reaching out to for two years bounds up to me in the playground and tells me she's so happy. I ask her if she's pregnant and she tells me no, it's because she's become a Christian! Or another friend who tells me over a coffee that he's changed from a church-goer to a 24/7 Christian. Or a man who for years has treated his family badly coming round to my home and asking if he can borrow my parenting magazines as he'd like to become a better father. Or the couple who asked for prayer in our Alpha group because the husband has had an affair. We all prayed and God did a miracle. At the next session they told us that past week had been like a second honeymoon and a few months later they became believers and were baptised. Watching on as prodigals return home and witnessing the power of God transforming lives, even though they might be few and far between, make the hard work and countless hours of investment worth more than all the gold in the world.'

Sarah's Story:

I grew up in a Christian home and we used to go to mass every Sunday. When I was eighteen I left home and put the faith issue behind me.

Several years later I was waiting for my little boy to come out of school and I met Richard and Riekje (who were also waiting for their son to come out of the same class). They told me that they were in Spain to start a new church. That got me thinking again about the whole issue of Jesus, church and community.

About a year later Riekje persuaded me to come along to their home group. I really liked the way everyone shared about their faith, and their doubts. I was frustrated because I wanted this personal relationship with Christ but felt I could not have one.

Sometime later Troy, another leader in the church, suggested that someone pray with me. So I asked him to stop talking and pray with me right then and there. Afterwards I had a picture of a circle of people from the church with outstretched hands. All I had to do was reach out and ask for help because I could not believe on my own. In particular Riekje has been the person who has led me through. It's not anything that she's said, but she's been by my side and just gently accompanied me on my search for Christ.

 For more information visit: www.mountainview-church.com

SOUL . . . IN THE CITY

CHURCH	SANCTUS1, MANCHESTER
DENOMINATION	ANGLICAN
CATEGORY	NEW CHURCH PLANT
LOCATION	CITY CENTRE

In June 1996, the IRA detonated a 3,300lb bomb in the heart of Manchester. The initial despair was replaced by the opportunist Mancunian attitude which meant the city centre was re-imagined, re-planned and changed forever.

The bomb was the catalyst for change, but coupled with this event there has also been a gradual movement of people back to the centre. In 1991 there were approximately one thousand residents but this figure has now increased to around twenty thousand and, perhaps most significantly, 80 per cent are aged between eighteen and forty. The area is now an attractive regional hub drawing young urbanites to live, work, shop and party.

In response to this dynamic situation, Manchester diocese appointed Ben Edson as the city centre missioner in July 2001. Ben's brief was to explore new ways of being church for this new residential community.

Sanctus1 started in October 2001 as a conversation between Ben and Ruth Edson and a young Christian couple. 'This couple,' says Ben, 'were passionately committed to their culture, to the city centre and to the Christian faith but had yet to find a church that affirmed their culture and recognised that God was present and active within it.' They met together every Wednesday night and began to explore the question of church; after a few weeks they realised that they *were* church. Sanctus1 had started. They continued to meet every Wednesday, selecting a time and day that they thought was accessible to the highly mobile city centre community. They also began to network and make contact with people in the city centre as they sought to establish a core community.

This couple . . . had yet to find a church that affirmed their culture and recognised that God was present and active within it

In February 2002 Sanctus1 had their first public act of worship, 'Sanctum', in Manchester Cathedral. The service was alternative worship and aimed to create a sacred space in the heart of the city. They decided to keep the pattern of a once monthly Sunday evening service and a weekly meeting on Wednesday.

Gradually Sanctus1 formed as a community. There were weeks when numbers were low but they remained faithful and carried on meeting. A website was launched, publicity material produced and people were invited to come along. Gradually and slowly Sanctus1 grew, the community sought authenticity rather than relevance and gradually an expression of church emerged that was culturally in tune with the city centre.

Autumn 2003 was a time of significant growth when the church doubled in size. This had an effect on the community and changed the pattern of meeting. 'The midweek meetings seek to build community and deliberately aim to be small with around fifteen to twenty people,' explains Ben, 'we therefore decided that Sanctus1 should be divided into two groups.' This enabled the church to have more capacity for growth and to develop a greater sense of belonging. Both groups decided to meet together once a month on a Wednesday to share a meal and to have a shared Eucharist.

The pattern since that time has evolved; there are now three midweek meetings, two on Wednesday and one on Tuesday. Sanctus1 also now has two Sunday services, an alternative worship service on the fourth Sunday and an intergeneration service on the second Sunday.

People naturally invite their friends and Sanctus1 grows

'The growth has continued principally as a result of word of mouth invitations and we now number approximately sixty people,' says Ben. 'People naturally invite their friends and Sanctus1 grows.'

> **A Member's Story:**
>
> Sanctus1 is the church I have always sought and never previously found. It's a community with whom I can be 'me', honest about my beliefs, questions, fears, hopes and dreams; it's where I feel accepted and affirmed for who I am, as I am.
>
> It's a church where difficult questions about God, faith, life and the world can be asked without receiving trite answers. The chance to reflect upon and wrestle with issues of life and faith in God's presence,

rather than simply being told what to believe and do, is sometimes challenging, but also hugely liberating and inspiring.

It is wonderful to be part of a community where God and the world, sacred and secular aren't boxed up neatly and separately but rather where life and faith are integrated, where God is recognised to be present and active in our lives and in all of creation, if we just listen and look. This is a place where Christ's love for all people and his passion for justice for the oppressed, is taken seriously as a model for our own lives as his disciples.

It's a church where I can worship God in creative ways, where we are not constantly bombarded by words but where there is space to listen for God's still, small voice . . . space to meet the living God and to be transformed by the encounter.

The church is engaged in mission in a number of innovative ways. For the past three years Sanctus1 has had a stand at the annual Mind, Body, Spirit Fair – a New Age event that attracts around eleven thousand people to Manchester G-MEX. In this space they offer Christian prayer for healing and share their faith with the spiritual searchers that they encounter.

Two regular events are held in the city centre: 'll' is a night of contemporary electronica music and creative media in a centrally located bar. It is a place for people who have no relationship with the church to come and meet informally with Sanctus1. They also co-ordinate and host a once monthly film night called 'Reel Spirituality'. People gather for food, watch a film and have a discussion to identify some of the spiritual themes and issues raised by what they have seen.

Recently, in partnership with The Methodist Church and City Centre Management the church has established 'Nexus'. This is a venue for work with minority groups as well as a place to express creative arts; there is also a night café here staffed by volunteers of Sanctus1. The night café offers a safe and alternative venue for those enjoying Manchester's night scene.

Ben says that 'Sanctus1 is a fragile, incomplete community, learning together about what it means to be church in a transient culture.'

  For more information visit: www.sanctus1.co.uk

CHURCH BEYOND WALLS

CHURCH	ELIM CHURCH, TAMWORTH
DENOMINATION	ELIM
CATEGORY	ESTABLISHED CHURCH, NEW INTEREST
LOCATION	TOWN CENTRE

Twelve years ago the Tamworth Elim Church had no regular contact with its community. Today on an average week, the lives of over a thousand people beyond the walls of the church are touched through its community outreach and the number of staff has increased from one to over twenty-five.

In 1994, a Day Nursery was started in its church building. In 1996, they purchased five adjacent, derelict houses and converted them into a community coffee shop, book shop, offices, meeting rooms and special needs housing. The Manna House Centre has since developed a Pregnancy Crisis Centre and a counselling service for the community.

'The problem with many church leaders is they overestimate what can be achieved in one year but underestimate what can be achieved in five years!' says Steve Jonathan, pastor of the Tamworth Elim Church. 'Whilst I am unsure where I first heard, or even read, these words, they continue to challenge me as a church leader to look at the longer term vision of our church.' He continues, 'It is so tempting for church leaders to look for "quick fixes", a magic wand or spiritual recipe that will bring instant success to the ministries of our churches but what is needed is a solid foundation that can steadily be build upon.'

The church is situated in a suburb of a market town of 75,000 and has been a small, but faithful witness to the community for over seventy years. However, about twelve years ago, there was an awareness that they had become stale and stagnant, hardly ever seeing a visitor come through their doors. 'Our Anglican neighbours were benefiting from their ready-made contacts through their many "hatches, matches and despatches",' says Steve. 'We quickly realised however, that we needed to be innovative in our approach and look for new ways to touch the heart of our community.'

We needed to win the right to share our message

The church decided three things were vital if they were to make an impact on their community. 'We needed to win the right to share our message by getting amongst our community and "rubbing shoulders" with irreligious people on a day-to-day basis,' says Steve. 'We also recognised the need to live authentic and genuine Christian lives in order to counter any accusation of hypocrisy. Finally we needed to present the Christian gospel clearly, without evangelical jargon or cliché and this is where we started.

'The desire to reach people with the gospel is the driving force and motivation of the leadership team and the church congregation. There are two extremes into which churches often fall, to preach a message that it is not lived out in practice, or to show compassion and perform good deeds without ever proclaiming and explaining the hope that we have. Our desire is to communicate the good news through words and deeds.' The mission statement 'to share the love of God with our community in word and deed' is the undergirding principle of the church.

Increased contacts and relationships with the community have provided the church with more opportunities to share the gospel. Over the last 12 years the congregation has steadily developed causing the problem of outgrowing the church building. A new building project is adding a fully equipped industrial kitchen to provide luncheons to the elderly, a community annex, a 64-place day nursery and an enlarged church auditorium.

'The last few years have certainly been an exciting journey of faith,' admits Steve. 'We are not a church with lots of money or affluent church members, so we have needed to trust the Lord to provide every step of the way. It has been thrilling to see so many organisations believe in and support our vision. It is also exhilarating to lead a team who are so faithful, loyal and flexible in their approach to church life. Thinking outside the box is simply second nature for them.'

In addition to all the usual services that a church provides, the Elim Church in Tamworth also offers a range of community services which include:

- Day Nursery for 64 children
- Special needs house for three adults

- Community coffee shop and book service
- Pregnancy Crisis Centre
- Counselling Service
- Schools programmes, including PSHE lessons in a range of subjects
- Luncheon and friendship club and social outreach amongst the elderly
- Drugs project
- Teaching English as a foreign language

The church continues to delight in what they regard as God's favour, continually looking out for new ways of reaching their community with the gospel in word and deed. The church leadership adamantly refuses to stand still or rest on their laurels but has an overwhelming desire to move forward in faith, daring to believe and choosing to be obedient to all that God has for them.

Pat and Joe's Story:

In July 2004, we attended Prime Time friendship and luncheon club; the welcome we received put us at ease immediately. We were very impressed with this local community over-sixties luncheon and friendship club run by the Elim Church. A few weeks later we decided to attend the Sunday morning celebration service; again we were impressed with Stephen (pastor) and Paul (associate pastor) and after four weeks we knew we wanted to be part of the church and become Christians. On Easter Sunday 2005, we both went to Stephen without each other knowing and prayed the prayer of commitment.

How our lives have changed since then! Our marriage has improved from good to great. We now read and discuss the Bible regularly together, seeking to put what we learn into practice. We are more calm, tolerant and considerate and seek to help people more often, especially those in need. All these things have happened because of our relationship with the Lord Jesus Christ and the Holy Spirit. We pray and thank God regularly for all the help we have received to become Christians.

 To find out more about Elim Church, Tamworth go to:
www.tamworth-elim.org.uk

B1 – MORE THAN A POSTCODE

CHURCH	*B1 CHURCH, BIRMINGHAM*
DENOMINATION	*CHURCH OF ENGLAND*
CATEGORY	*NETWORK CHURCH*
LOCATION	*CITY CENTRE*

Exhausting, stimulating, challenging, stretching, problematic and exciting are all words that Geoff Lanham, leader of B1 Church in Birmingham, uses to describe the rollercoaster journey of the last six years.

Exhausting, stimulating, challenging, stretching, problematic and exciting With a brief to engage in network evangelism among non-churched people in their twenties and thirties, a core team, mostly from St John's Church, Harborne, began to draw together in December 2000. 'We knew we wanted to be a church for three categories of people,' explains Geoff. 'Those with little or no background in Christian understanding, those who couldn't relate to or fit into existing church culture and those who were spiritually interested, but not religious.'

COMMUNITY

The name B1 was chosen partly because it's the postcode of central Birmingham, but also because it spoke of the value that this new church wanted to place on being community. 'We wanted to create a church in which people felt comfortable belonging before they were required to behave or believe the right things,' says Geoff. 'Conversion to community might well occur before conversion to Jesus.'

NETWORK

B1 calls itself a network church because parish boundaries are becoming increasingly anachronistic in large towns and cities. People now live, work, relax, socialise and worship in a variety of different communities or locations. The idea is that those who try it out will have interests and friendships in common but not necessarily geographical proximity. Within three years the church grew to 60 adults but since then there have been ups and downs due to the mobile lifestyles of the people they are working with.

STRATEGY

B1's initial strategy was to run events hosted in neutral venues to create environments of genuine engagement and dialogue with non-churched people. They met in pubs and bars with an aim of facilitating conversation about Jesus Christ that otherwise would not happen. In the first two years they clearly saw that happening but began to realise that they were drifting into being too event-driven, the cost of which was the burden of being continually creative and burn-out. 'We've learned that effectiveness has to be more than just measuring attendance at formal gatherings,' explains Geoff and he goes on to say that 'putting all our energies into servicing events hindered our capacity to build relationships, so we've had to go back to reminding ourselves of our key values of credibility and reality in our relationships.' A one-to-one approach to discipleship has been found to be the only viable option due to the difficulty of running a course with just a trickle of new believers.

A one-to-one approach to discipleship has been found to be the only viable option

More recently, B1 has concentrated on developing informal interactions within their networks by encouraging people to give time to what they naturally enjoy doing and promoting smaller scale initiatives from the ground up. Wine tasting, jazz nights, 5-a-side football, a canal boat trip and meeting in Balti houses demonstrates some of the ways that they have gone back to their roots in terms of creating community and enjoying open edged socialising.

Creativity in worship has been a key value for B1. They have had a commitment to experiment with giving people more choice about how they interact in worship and leaving more room for questioning and discussion. 'Like it or not, consumerism profoundly shapes the way we think about life,' comments Geoff. 'Being told what to do at every stage is anathema to the type of people we're hoping to reach.' Having run a variety of courses and events, they have learned that even short programmes don't really fit the culture of those working in the city centre as they find it very hard to commit to attend. So a dream for the future is to find a venue that will enable them to create an 'oasis type' imaginative, sacred space in the city centre that could be available for workers to drop into at lunchtimes or after work. The idea would be to offer some 'reflective headspace' and a gentle introduction to God's peace and presence using multimedia resources.

a safe place in which to express questions, doubts and alternative viewpoints without fear of judgement

B1 has been described as a safe place in which to express questions, doubts and alternative viewpoints without fear of judgement. Geoff makes the point that 'the Lord seems to be giving us this role of engaging in dialogue with people who've fallen out of the boat, but have retained vestiges of a private faith. A number have found a safe home with us; however, when you emphasise belonging and acceptance it can mean that you have to accept a slight diffusion of your mission focus in some areas. We are certainly a heterogeneous bunch, so holding together the twin values of unity and diversity has been a challenge. It's not always easy to keep an outward focus while ensuring that enough attention is paid to building up community life.'

So what has Geoff discovered on the journey so far?

'I've discovered that you never stop feeling fragile. Life is a bit like a cliff walk along the coastal path in Cornwall. You gain height and then lose it, gain some more and descend again. The trick is to enjoy the view at each stage. Maybe we'll only see a few people go from the very beginning of their journey through to mature following. We don't kid ourselves that results will be instant or dramatic. We know we're in mission for the long haul. B1 is one small, fragile experiment. It won't be "the answer" to mission in post-modern times and other experiments will need to be contextualised among different subcultures.'

John and Sarah (not their real names) are now regular attenders at B1. They had a developing friendship with a couple in the church, because of work connections. Back in 2001-02 they began to come to a few events. John began to play football with them on a Monday night. An invitation to become godparents proved the trigger for beginning to come to Sunday services. They now help with the children's work and belong to a midweek small group. Their exciting spiritual growth has developed out of an enjoyment of belonging to our community and making new friends.

In their own words they describe the value of their church experience:

'B1 is informal, friendly, modern and everything we could not find in conventional church . . . for us it provides a great sense of well-being and belonging. We appreciate meeting people who are non-judgemental, who accept that you can get closer to God at your own pace and that you are on your own individual spiritual journey – this is a major strength of B1. People accept you for who you are, what you are and where you are going, be it the first step or the final rung of the ladder.'

For more information visit: www.b1church.net

BRIDGING THE GAP

CHURCH	*THE BRIDGE, BURBAGE*
DENOMINATION	*METHODIST*
CATEGORY	*NEW CHURCH PLANT*
LOCATION	*SUBURBAN*

'Because Church can be relevant' – is the strap-line for The Bridge, a church that describes itself as 'a community, with activities for all ages, communicating the Christian message through hospitality, in an accessible, relaxed and informal setting.'

About forty to sixty meet regularly on a Sunday at 5 p.m. in a local secondary school in Burbage, Leicestershire for a presentation of the gospel and community building time. This is a dispersed network; many are members of small groups meeting for word, worship and witness, but who also meet for meals, sports and socials. Being part of the wider Methodist Connexion in Hinckley, the circuit employs a part-time lay worker to lead The Bridge team.

THE ETHOS

'We are a church for people who are not really into church,' explains Tim Lea, leader of The Bridge. 'We are more into kingdom than denominations, more into people than programmes, more into building community and hospitality than meetings, more into mission than maintenance, more into discipleship than conversion and more into belonging than doctrine.'

We are a church for people who are not really into church

The Bridge sums up their ethos with the following values:
• Non-judgemental
• Hospitable
• Fun
• Informal
• Relevant

- Experimental
- Person centred
- Genuine
- Personal
- Friendly

'We believe that following Jesus is a story we need to live out with integrity 24/7,' says Tim. 'It is about everyday life, where there is no secular/sacred divide. We try to share the gospel in a language that is accessible, jargon free and easy to understand.' Events at The Bridge make use of drama, contemporary Christian and non-Christian live music, video/DVD clips, meditations and PowerPoint presentations.

CONNECTING

The church aims to connect with the local community in a variety of ways:

- Incarnationally – members of The Bridge seek to live out their faith in the workplace, at home and through their leisure activities.

- Evangelistically – through the following programmes: Alpha in the local pub, a highly successful children's holiday club, Friday night badminton club, small groups, discipleship mentoring and dropping The Bridge DVD presentation through letterboxes.

- Socially – by serving the local community in a variety of initiatives.

The church's website keeps both members and inquirers up to date about what is going on.

Tim says, 'We have never purposefully set out to reach those who have drifted away from church, but interestingly that's just what has happened. Our way of "being church" has been attractive to the prodigals as we have become a place of healing, a safe place to explore and a resting place. There has been a positive ripple-like effect for other churches in the area through The Bridge's way of "being church".'

THE STORY

The Bridge was started just over ten years ago with a relatively blank sheet of paper. The challenge was to work out how to 'do church' differently. A great deal of prayer and creative thought went into developing the structure of what exists today and they discovered that

The Bridge is about building relationships, building confidence and building disciples

if they started with mission then church would follow. 'The Bridge is about building relationships, building confidence and building disciples,' says Tim. 'Our children's work is not just about knowledge but about a walk with God - a lived out practical earthy spirituality.'

THE HIGHLIGHTS

'It has been hard work over those ten years,' admits Tim. 'There has been blood, sweat and tears . . . *but* . . . when asked if the team would do it again, knowing what they now know, they all answered with a resounding "YES". We have made mistakes but it has been about acknowledging them, solving them and moving on. The best things are being part of a team, growing and maturing as disciples, being surprised by God and seeing him at work in the world.'

Male, thirty-nine-year-old telecoms worker:

Two years ago I felt like ending it all. My marriage was on the rocks because of mutual ignorance of each other's wants and needs. We had moved house twice in a year, I had to live away from home for 12 months and my mother died two months after we moved the second time. I didn't care any more.

Several weeks later I was watching a play at The Bridge and dreading going home, when I saw a bright flash in my eye. After contemplating this I decided, given my current state, that it may well be God saying: 'OK bud, come with me, let's sort this out.'

It took several weeks to sort myself out mentally – I had rather fallen to pieces in the previous months. Since then I have viewed life in a very different, better way. I feel comfortable with myself and my relationship with my wife has never been better. After several discussions she has also changed and we are both the better for it.

We went to New Wine which was fantastic; my whole attitude is that in whatever I do, I don't have to do it alone.

 For more information visit: www.thebridgeonline.co.uk

SEEKING NEW HORIZONS

CHURCH	*NEW HORIZONS, HEMEL HEMPSTEAD*
DENOMINATION	*INDEPENDENT*
CATEGORY	*CAFÉ CHURCH*
LOCATION	*SUBURBAN*

Over its seven-year history, New Horizons Christian Fellowship has employed various means of reaching out to the town of Hemel Hempstead. Hand delivering thousands of glossy postcards publicising special events and inviting friends and neighbours along has been one method, but in the summer of 2005 they tried something quite different.

Writing and recording a worship CD, *Marvellous Things*, from scratch they then hand-delivered 35,000 copies as a free gift to the town. The result? Dozens of newcomers attended a special celebration service. Some decided to stay; some decided this wasn't really their thing. 'In simple terms,' says church member Harvey Fryer, 'we had hoped and believed for a huge influx which hasn't transpired, at least not as yet. Instead we are finding people who have listened to *Marvellous Things* and feel attracted to a church that is attracted to its community.'

'In many ways our church is both different and the same. Meeting in a community centre we look different to other churches with our "café-style" tables and chairs, but also feel a bit different as people are encouraged to eat and drink throughout the service.' Harvey goes on to make the point that 'it's more natural for us to see each other's faces than to look at the back of people's heads' and claims that café-services also encourage a more social church: 'Tables tend to break the "this is my seat" mentality of traditional church.' Upbeat music and practical messages dealing with real life issues are very much on the agenda and New Horizons promises that 'what you learn on the weekend, you'll be able to use during the week.' 'So we're just doing what cafés and pubs have always done; providing a comfortable, welcoming environment where everyone feels at home.'

Harvey says that their relaxed atmosphere reflects their mission statement:

'The Spirit of the Lord is on me, because he has anointed me to preach good news to the poor. He has sent me to proclaim freedom for the prisoners and recovery of sight for the blind, to release the oppressed, to proclaim the year of the Lord's favour.' (Lk. 4:18, NIV)

'We want to reach out to those in need, providing them with a non-threatening environment where they have the opportunity to experience a love they may never have known.'

> We want to reach out to those in need, providing them with a non-threatening environment where they have the opportunity to experience a love they may never have known

New Horizons is a church that loves its community. 'The fact we meet in a community centre is a strategic decision,' explains Harvey. 'Being part of the community means we do what the community loves to do - and when it comes to passions in Hemel Hempstead, well, football scores pretty highly.' That is why for one week they do away with the usual Sunday morning service and host a community football tournament. Recently they saw 700 people visiting the event during the day when families and young footballers came together for a free, fun event with no catches or evangelistic strategies. The church logo was on display and all of the members had name labels, 'but what we are really looking to show off,' says Harvey, 'is a God who is into leisure, togetherness, community and relaxation. We passionately believe that all those things are close to the heart of our Creator.'

Responding to needs is central to the life of the church, but while they are keen to adapt the way they do things to meet the challenges around them, they are careful that their core beliefs are explained clearly at the earliest opportunity. Introduction evenings help newcomers to learn more about the church and find out how they can become involved.

While Pastor Arno Steen Andreasen is responsible for the spiritual direction of the church, New Horizons believes in sharing responsibility for decision-making. The church is made up of Ministry Teams of church members who 'make things happen'. 'We're keen for committed Christians to become involved in our ministry groups which oversee key areas of church life such as events, fellowship and worship services,' says Harvey. 'These groups are responsible for budgets that they are free to use in whichever way they choose, and can make key decisions. Anyone at church who has attended an introduction course, and actively involved in the activity can join these groups, the only further stipulation being that the decision-making should be in line with the church's mission, vision, theology and values of the church.'

Currently about seventy people regularly attend the church, this number is swelled by the 'WorldShapers Academy' – students who join each year from across the globe to study for an Applied Theology Associate degree which is led by pastor Arno Steen Andreasen.

'We're hardly a mega church,' says Harvey, 'just one that is passionate about the people it meets during day-to-day life. We believe it's about showing an interest in individual lives, rather than putting on a show to attract people. At the end of the day, what we're doing isn't out of the reach of any other church. We're just following a formula that works because it's God's way of doing things – reaching out to the people we meet.'

Jess's Story:

Life hasn't been the same since I became involved in New Horizons Christian Fellowship. It was with trepidation that I first opened the doors to the church, but that same day I left with excitement and a sense of belonging. The easygoing and informal café style enabled me to quickly build solid relationships. I was amazed by the warmth and enthusiasm with which I was welcomed and received.

New Horizons has truly become my family. It's so much more than a Sunday service; it's an integral part of my social and spiritual life. The gospel-reading group has given me a passion to delve deeper into the Bible; we have down-to-earth, real-life discussions that help me to apply God's word to everyday situations. After only three months, I feel supported and loved and enjoy being involved in it, particularly the youth work. I am excited about being a part of God's future plans for the church and look forward to seeing more of its impact on the community. God is doing awesome things at New Horizons and I feel privileged to be involved in this!

For more information visit: www.nhcf.org.uk

CHURCH FOR EXPLORERS

CHURCH	*EXPLORE, BRACKNELL*
DENOMINATION	*BAPTIST*
CATEGORY	*SEEKER/CONGREGATIONAL PLANT*
LOCATION	*SUBURBAN*

You grab a doughnut and a coffee, sit back and relax. No one puts pressure on you and you can make up your own mind about the things you are looking at. Contemporary arts, music, drama and multimedia are all used to see what God has to say about real-life issues.

'Explore: Life' is just one facet of the Explore congregation, part of Easthampstead Baptist Church in Bracknell.

Following some demographic research in the year 2000 it was decided to establish a new congregation giving it the remit of attracting unchurched eighteen to thirty-five year- olds. In Bracknell over 50 per cent of the population fall into this age range and very few of them go to church.

A core team of 12 began to meet to study the Bible, pray and plan together. A mission statement was agreed: 'To introduce people to the love of God and encourage them to become devoted followers of Christ.' Five core values of Community, Communication, Commitment, Caring and Celebrating were also developed to help shape what the new congregation might look like.

The name 'Explore' was decided upon and at the beginning of 2003 'Explore: Life' – a seeker-targeted programme run in a local sports centre, was launched.

PASSION . . .

Chris Porter leader of Explore says: 'We value and love non-Christians, we have a passion to reach them, to serve them and to appreciate them. We want non-Christians to feel a part of our community, to belong to it and to own it.' With the exception of the teaching ministry, those who are not yet Christians are involved in everything that Explore does whether it be playing in the band, helping with the children's work, being part of one of the technical teams or organising social events. The challenge is for each believer to be praying

We want non-Christians to feel a part of our community, to belong to it and to own it

for and with their non-Christian friends, to practically support and help them, to invite them to events and to love them unconditionally.

> **A single mum** is moving house. She can't afford a removals van, but two of her friends show up on the day of the move and bring with them two others each with their own cars. They don't know this mum and she doesn't know them but they come nonetheless. They have all given up their one day off in the week to show up and hump furniture and boxes. They make numerous trips with cars jam packed full of stuff. It takes all day and they finish by delivering a box full of food and household necessities. The mum is bowled over. Who are these people and why would they do this? So she begins to investigate and turns up one Sunday at her friend's church. She receives a warm welcome and sees the people who helped her move; her young child is included and loved despite his enthusiastic noise production. The music is lively and contemporary and she recognises it from the radio, there are things to watch on a big screen and the talk has relevance to her life. She carries on coming and is baptised 18 months later; her father approaches a church leader at the end of that service offering all the thanks he can. She is a changed person and he can see God at work in her; there are tears in his eyes . . . this is church.

GROWTH . . .

The original group of 12 has now grown to around fifty adults who regularly attend today. The children's work - Explorers - has also grown from six children to over twenty. Around 60 per cent of the growth has come from non-church people and over 80 per cent has been within their target age range.

A number of those joining have had some church backgound in the past but for one reason or another have stopped attending. Some have had very negative experiences of high pressure evangelistic activities; others have been hurt by the church and some just drifted away because they found it irrelevant and boring.

CONNECTING . . .

Chris emphasises that the congregation connects with people through friendships. 'We encourage people to build relationships and then we try to provide high quality social and seeker-targeted events for them to invite their friends to. We aim to do this not just for adults, but for children too.'

> There is a man who struggles with an addiction, he is invited by his neighbour to come with her to church – she is an older lady and she doesn't really find the services very helpful, too loud and not her style but she brings him anyway. She realises that it's not about her, it's about the man – and he loves it. He connects with a small group who decide to throw a birthday party for him, someone in the group bakes a cake, others get presents and still others throw open their home to host the evening organising great food and drink. He comes and has the most amazing time; afterwards with tears in his eyes he admits that despite being in his mid-thirties he can never remember a birthday when someone got him a cake; all he has wanted all these years is a birthday with a cake. God prompted that small group to give him a party – bake him a birthday cake. God is at work . . . this is church.

DISCIPLESHIP . . .

A commonly held assumption of churches that emphasise reaching seekers is that they must be weak on discipleship. 'We believe this to be untrue,' responds Chris, 'in fact we think it is totally the opposite, discipleship is about becoming more like the person of Jesus. As we seek to grow in our love for non-Christians, as we seek to serve sacrificially, as we debate and discuss "real life" issues in events and in small groups and as we try to serve our local community, practically caring for people in need, we are growing to be more like Jesus.'

Discipleship is about becoming more like the person of Jesus

For more information visit: www.ebc-bracknell.org/explore

POSTSCRIPT

At the beginning of this section we emphasised that we were not looking for or promoting a definitive model of what a twenty-first century church should look like.

As you have read these stories you will have undoubtedly concluded, as we have done, that there is no blueprint, no pattern to follow, no certain or quick method that will make your church grow. What they do show however is that God loves variety, is infinitely creative and takes pleasure in seeing his children step out in faith and 'have a go'.

As you will be aware, we have not tried to form a definitive list of what is working; you will doubtless know of many different examples yourself. Neither do we claim they are the best in their field of ministry but they are stories of people who have been prepared to be vulnerable and share their experiences in the hope that others might be encouraged and inspired to do something 'extraordinary' for God.

We would like to conclude however, by highlighting a number of recurring values either specified or implied throughout this section, many of which you will recognise from the first section of the book.

RELATIONSHIP

Everything we seek to do stands or falls on the issue of relationship. We can have the best programme available but if there is no real personal interaction with those we are trying to reach we cannot succeed. The building and nurturing of genuine friendships is central to effective faith-sharing.

BELONGING

In the context of the stories, belonging means welcoming people into the heart of our community whether or not they are ready to believe. This may include close involvement in the life and activities of the church; it may also raise difficult questions for those in leadership. What is evident though is that people are much more likely to stay if they feel valued and needed.

RELEVANCE

In a world where the default image of the church is one of crushing boredom and utter irrelevancy, the need to contextualise the gospel has never been more pressing. Churches have to work hard at keeping this high up the agenda because the Christian default is set to return to what we are comfortable and secure with, which is often light years away from those with whom we are trying to connect.

JOURNEY

This theme is evident throughout the stories. Many 'not yet believers' recognise that they are on a spiritual journey which, rather than delivering them to an instant destination, will gradually lead them to faith. Churches are increasingly aware that evangelism is not just about bringing people to a crisis decision but accompanying and guiding them as they travel a road of discovery.

CONSISTENCY

An interesting observation when taking the stories as a whole is the importance attached to long-term commitment of ministry. Few churches see rapid results, most recognise that they are in it for the long haul and, not surprisingly, none claim it has been easy! A gradual building of trust between the community and the local church is clearly an essential element in any form of outreach.

AUTHENTICITY

One of the most common charges levelled at believers, usually unjustly so, is that of hypocrisy. It's not surprising therefore that many churches list living authentic Christian lifestyles as a non-negotiable value. This is true both in a personal and corporate context. Those who do not yet believe need to know that what they see in the public arena is matched by what is seen in the personal one and vice-versa.

ACCEPTANCE

Perhaps one of the most contentious areas in the church today revolves around the issue of what is 'acceptable' and what isn't. The line between welcoming those with 'baggage' without condoning behaviour that may be anything but 'Christian' is a fine one requiring grace and discernment at the highest level. It is clear that when churches take seriously the command to 'go into all the world' then they are quickly faced with pastoral situations they would probably never encounter if they just stayed at home!

VISION

A common theme in the stories is that of vision. Many of the new initiatives began out of God giving a dream, a hope, a spiritual ambition to someone. This highlights the importance of having the right people in the right place at the right time and then creating a team around them who are able to turn those dreams into reality.

COURAGE

A recurring theme throughout the stories is that of boldness. Being prepared to try something new 'against the odds' and maybe against the wishes of some can be immensely challenging. It's probably true that those who are stretched the most tend to grow the best. The possibility of failure is never far way from courage – but 'how much better to have tried and failed than to never have tried at all' – to misquote someone!

PRAYER

Prayer is undoubtedly seen as the key throughout the stories listed in this section of the book. This of course takes many forms; some prayed for long periods before beginning a work, others found themselves in the midst of something new and quickly recognised their need to call out to God for help and direction. However, what is clear is that nothing of substance can hope to be achieved without a living reliance on our heavenly Father.

> 'Now faith is being sure of what we hope for and certain of what we do not see.' (Heb. 11:1, NIV)

This verse seems to sum up much of what has been explored throughout these pages.

These stories demonstrate faith in a God that has not given up on his creation but is passionate about revealing himself in a way that this generation can relate to and recognise. Although techniques and models of ministry will always be changing, his love remains constant and available to all.

We hope this book has been of help and an inspiration to you.

If RUN can serve you in any way in your ministry, please do get in touch with us.

RUN is a non-denominational network of many hundreds of members who are discovering what it means to be church in twenty-first century society and who share a passion to reach people for Christ in a culture that has largely given up on religion.

Since 1994 RUN has held firmly to its core values:

- Envisioning
- Resourcing
- Networking

By aiming to keep at the leading edge of outreach initiatives, RUN is well placed to help equip leaders for the task of developing effective, missional churches. Regular conferences, workshops and training events are held with input from the highest quality thinkers and practitioners.

Access to an extensive database of multi-media and drama resources is a major benefit of membership with instant downloads available from the member's section of the website. Members are also encouraged to submit material that they have produced for the benefit of others. Networking with other likeminded members provides inspiration, as ideas and experiences are shared through the directory and forum.

RUN is a member of the Evangelical Alliance and is committed to working in partnership with all who share similar vision and values, believing that so much more can be achieved together than alone.

If you would like more information about RUN visit:
www.run.org.uk

Or contact:
RUN
PO Box 387
Aylesbury
Bucks
HP21 8WH
T: 0870 787 3635
E: info@run.org.uk

EMERGINGCHURCH.INFO

Emergingchurch.info is a website sharing stories, reflections and discussion from fresh expressions of church. It is widely regarded as something of an online hub for the emerging church community in the UK and wider afield.

The stories and reflections on the site are all from people 'being church' rather than distant observers and reflect a wide range of experiences – from embryonic groups to established churches. Stories of celebration and growth but also frustration and failure lend the site an honest and organic feel with no agenda other than to offer a wider audience to those who submit their stories. The evolution of the emerging church can also be seen as contributors regularly try to put into words the theology and theory of what is happening as people seek to celebrate and work out Christian faith in contemporary culture. People often respond to previous articles with fresh insights or visit the site and find themselves inspired to write of their experiences thus giving the site a genuine momentum and vitality.

Launched in October 2003, the site currently receives over ten thousand visitors per month from around the world.

www.emergingchurch.com

Fresh Expressions is an initiative of the Archbishops of Canterbury and York supported by the Methodist Council of Great Britain. Our aim is to resource a growing movement of fresh expressions of church across every diocese and district and ecumenically. We work across four key areas renewing vision, gathering news, supporting growth and developing training. The team are available for training days and conferences. Full details at www.freshexpressions.org.uk

expressions: the dvd

STORIES OF CHURCH FOR A CHANGING CULTURE

A DVD is available featuring eight of the stories used in this book.

This resource is jointly produced by RUN, Fresh Expressions and the Methodist Church and includes 14 video diaries of about 6 minutes each.

There is also a more in-depth look at some of the churches, lasting about 25 minutes and introduced by Diane Louise Jordan.

For more information or to obtain a copy please visit www.run.org.uk or contact:

RUN
PO Box 387
Aylesbury
Bucks
HP21 8WH
T: 0870 787 3635
E: info@run.org.uk